Understanding Depression

Understanding Health and Sickness Series
Miriam Bloom, Ph.D.
General Editor

Understanding Depression

Patricia Ainsworth, M.D.

University Press of Mississippi
Jackson

www.upress.state.ms.us

Copyright © 2000 by University Press of Mississippi
Manufactured in the United States of America

07   06   05   04   03   02   01   00   4   3   2

∞

Illustrations by Regan Causey Tuder.

Library of Congress Cataloging-in-Publication Data

Ainsworth, Patricia, M.D.
    Understanding depression / Patricia Ainsworth.
        p.   cm.—(Understanding health and sickness series)
    Includes bibliographical references and index.
    ISBN 1-57806-168-7 (cloth : alk. paper)—ISBN 1-57806-169-5
(pbk. : alk. paper)
    1. Depression, Mental.   2. Affective disorders.   I. Title.
II. Series.
    RC537.A39   2000
    616.85'27—dc21   99-35416
                                                          CIP

British Library Cataloging-in-Publication Data available

Contents

Acknowledgments

I am indebted to Dr. John Norton of the University of Mississippi Medical Center for critically reviewing the first draft of this manuscript and to Mrs. Martha A. McLendon for her suggestions concerning improvement of its general readability. Dr. Garth Bissette of the University of Mississippi Medical Center provided time, information, and insight regarding the final chapter on research. Dr. Richard E. Weddle and Owen A. Weddle supplied the original photographs and continuous support for the project. I am also grateful to Dr. Miriam Bloom for her guidance and patience.

Introduction

A physician contemplating suicide describes depression: "There's no crispness to the morning. The smell of coffee serves only as a reminder that another long, dreary day has begun. There's no real feeling, no joy, not even much anger, only emptiness. It's difficult to remember feeling any different and getting more difficult to go on feeling this way. Sitting in a dark corner with eyes closed imagining nothingness until there is nothing would be easier. Instead here's the day to face, the responsibilities, the people, the emptiness, but the energy that once fortified the day is no more. Concentration has become a bad joke. Even love is now only a faint echo of itself. A leaden haze obscures the day and folds into a dark tunnel with no hint of light at the end. Where is hope? There is none. Where is happiness? Gone as if it had never been, replaced by tears that must be hidden. Where is relief? Perhaps in death."

Depression is not moodiness. Moodiness is a transient, unpleasant feeling that often occurs in association with some physical or environmental irritant, and it is never debilitating. Depression is to moodiness as a hurricane is to a whirlwind.

Depression is a serious, sometimes chronic, and too often terminal physical illness that clouds the minds of sufferers, robs them of joy and peace, wreaks havoc with their appetites and sleep patterns, and leaves their bodies vulnerable to physical illness and to death either self-inflicted or as a result of medical illness. One of the most common illnesses found in human beings, depression afflicts 20 percent of the population in the United States and worldwide. Women are two to three times more likely to fall victim to this mood disorder than are men. Depression is an equal opportunity offender, exempting no one on the basis of age, sex, race, religion, sexual orientation, or nation of origin.

The causes of depression have not been clearly defined. Research points to biological abnormalities in the brain and in the chemicals that transmit messages through the brain. Many clinicians subscribe to the "fertile ground" theory, which holds that someone who is at risk for depression must have a hereditary or physical vulnerability to the condition that causes the mood-regulating system to fail when life's stresses exceed the person's ability to cope with them. In other words, there must be a fertile field in which the weeds of stress can prosper and grow.

One point is certain. Depression is not a sign of character weakness; it is a total body illness. People with serious depressive disorders cannot pull themselves together and get on with it. They must struggle to meet life's everyday demands. They suffer from the illness itself, from a loss of self-confidence, and ultimately from the misapprehensions of well-meaning people around them. Some live through it with or without help, but others die. The cost to families, friends, and society is immeasurable. In dollars alone, the cost of depression in the United States runs into the billions each year. The toll is far too high, especially when effective treatment is available for most sufferers.

Depression is an old illness, not a recent affliction spawned by the stresses of modern civilization. Remarkably detailed descriptions of depressive maladies can be found in the texts of ancient civilizations including China, Babylon, Egypt, India, and Greece. One of the best early descriptions of depression is in the Old Testament. In 1 Samuel 16:14, King Saul's mental suffering is ascribed to an "evil spirit . . . [that] troubled him." His suffering was relieved when he listened to David playing the harp—one of the earliest descriptions of music therapy. Later, when facing defeat in battle and the death of his sons, King Saul begged his manservant to relieve him of his anguish by killing him. When the manservant refused, Saul committed suicide (1 Samuel 31: 2–4).

Earlier in the same book (1 Samuel 1:2–20) we find the story of Hannah, a woman whose severe depression caused her to weep, fret, grieve, eat poorly, and be of sorrowful spirit. Her depression was attributed to her inability to conceive a child. Her prayers for a child were heard by a holy man who reassured her that the God of Israel would grant her plea. Afterward, Hannah was reassured and her mood improved so that she "went her way, and did eat, and her countenance was no more sad" (I Samuel 1:18). Shortly thereafter she conceived the child who would later be known as King Samuel.

Depression has affected many accomplished and productive public figures, including Peter Tchaikovsky, Vincent van Gogh, Abraham Lincoln, Vivien Leigh, Marilyn Monroe, Sylvia Plath, Primo Levi, John Lennon, Mike Wallace, Barry Manilow, and Diana, Princess of Wales. The fact that depression can run in families is tragically demonstrated by the Hemingways—Ernest, his father, his actress-granddaughter Margaux, and her eldest sister, all of whom suffered severe depression and all of whom but the last ultimately committed suicide. Well-known movie and television actress Patty Duke publicly acknowledged her bouts with mood disorder in an effort to promote better understanding of the condition and to encourage sufferers to "come out of the closet" and seek help. The world is full of physicians, attorneys, teachers, politicians, ministers, rabbis, priests, accountants, secretaries, supermarket managers, mothers, fathers, sons, and daughters who battle depression.

The best way to overcome an enemy is first to understand its nature. This book explores the nature of the enemy we call depression. We begin with a discussion of the symptoms of the illness, the impact it has on the lives of sufferers and those around them, and the most common types. We will see that depression may assume various guises in different groups of people, such as children, women following childbirth, and the elderly. Next, we elaborate on the idea of depression as a total body illness, noting the medical conditions commonly associated with it. Then we explore the causes of depression and the ways in which the illness can be managed by doctors as well as by sufferers and those who care for them. Hope is one of the most effective tools for combating a fierce enemy, and in the final chapter we discuss some of the promising research possibilities for new and improved means by which this ancient foe may be overcome.

The resources reviewed during the preparation of this book included publications of the National Institute of Mental Health. The Internet allowed me access to many international articles about research on depression. I frequently consulted *Psychiatry* (W. B. Saunders Company, 1997), an excellent textbook for physicians edited by Allen Tasman, M.D., Jerald Kay, M.D., and Jeffrey A. Lieberman, M.D.

Understanding Depression

1. What Is Depression?

"I treated depression throughout my career and never really understood what it was I was treating until I suffered from depression myself."

—A psychiatrist

The innocuous-sounding word "depression" refers to a potentially disabling illness that affects many but is understood by few. Sufferers often do not realize the nature of their terrible malaise until they are so devastated that they can no longer help themselves, or they may recognize what they have been through only after they are on their way out of the shadows. The reason is simple. Depression is a sneak thief, slipping into a life gradually and robbing it of meaning, one loss at a time. The losses are imperceptible at first, but eventually weigh so heavily that the person's life becomes empty. Once begun, the course of depression varies with the individual and with the form of the illness. Untreated, it can last weeks, months, or even years.

In the general population, as many as one in five individuals may eventually suffer a significant depressive illness, although most will not seek treatment. During any year, one in ten people experience the sluggishness of mind, body, and spirit we know as depression. The risk is about the same in prepubertal boys and girls, but the ratio alters in adulthood, with females twice as likely as males to become depressed. This two-to-one ratio exists regardless of racial, ethnic, or economic background and has been reported in several countries.

Although depression can occur in very young children, even in those under five years of age, it is more likely to occur for the first time during teenage years or in early adulthood. Depression can also occur for the first time in midlife or later.

Depression tends to run in families. Children of depressed parents have a twofold-to-threefold greater risk of developing depression than children of nondepressive parents. Studies of families with histories of depression in many of their members support the theory that predisposition to depression can be inherited. Since the family tendency could be explained by similar environments rather than by genes, twins who have been adopted outside their biological families and reared apart have been studied with regard to risk for depression. Most of those studies show that if one identical twin (identical twins share the same genes) suffers from depression, the second twin will have a 70 percent chance of also becoming depressed, while the risk for siblings who are not identical twins is only about 25 percent. If heredity were the only factor, the shared rate of depression in identical twins would be 100 percent. Since this is not the case, genetics cannot be the only factor involved. At this point, no single gene has been identified as the culprit in causing depression, and it is more likely that several genes are involved.

According to the fertile ground theory, heredity and environment collude to cause depression. Environmental factors that may be important in causing depression include loss of a parent early in life, separation or divorce of parents, rearing patterns, abuse, low socioeconomic class, and recent life stresses.

Costs of Depression

Approximately one in five adults in the United States will suffer from depression at some time. Depression affects more than 17 million Americans each year. Mood disorders, including mania and various forms of depression, account for as many as 70 percent of psychiatric hospitalizations.

Sufferers of depression include some of the most creative and productive members of society, which means that the direct and indirect costs of this common illness are very high. The latest National Institutes of Health (U.S.) study on the cost of depression, reported for 1990, estimated the cost of depressive illness in the United States at between $33 billion and $44 billion annually (fig. 1.1), including direct treatment costs ($12.4 billion), absenteeism ($11.7 billion), lost productivity ($12.1 billion), and mortality costs ($7.5 billion). The number of lost work days due to depression may be as high as 200 million days per year.

On a more personal level, patients treated in psychiatric hospitals for serious depression may find themselves billed $1,000 to $1,500 a day or more for a hospitalization that may exceed five to seven days and occasionally last several weeks. Those charges may not even include the costs of physician visits, consultants, or special studies such as antidepressant medication blood levels or brain scans.

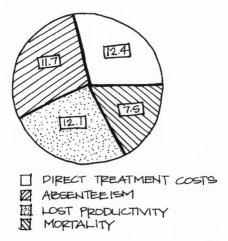

FIG. 1.1. Estimated annual cost of depression in the United States (in billions of dollars).

Most people, even solid middle-class individuals with good health insurance, will find themselves psychiatrically indigent if they require hospitalization for the treatment of depression. Health insurance policies, even good ones, commonly discriminate against psychiatric illness. Many policies have a poorer reimbursement rate for mental disorders, impose a lifetime maximum reimbursement limit (sometimes as little as $50,000), and require larger copayments for psychiatric treatment. The length-of-stay allowances for inpatient care of seriously depressed patients may also place the patient at significant risk. For example, a psychiatrist recently hospitalized a severely depressed woman on an emergency basis following her suicide attempt by overdose of prescribed medications. The insurance company ruled that the patient had to be discharged the day she no longer reported suicidal intent. The fragility of severely depressed patients in early recovery, including their increased risk for suicide, was apparently not a cost-efficient consideration.

Another problem is the stigma associated with mental illness, which can make treatment for depression and other brain disorders that are labeled as mental illnesses costly in personal ways. Traditionally, people with mental illnesses such as depression have been required to report their disorders on applications for a driver's license, for employment, for security clearance, and for other routine purposes, while people with other medical conditions generally have not. Although the recent federal Americans with Disabilities Act attempted to correct that form of discrimination, the problem remains. When a physician recently changed her medical liability insurance policy, the application asked whether the applicant had ever been treated for mental illness. Nowhere on the policy was there another question about any other medical illness or treatment. Fearing discrimination in hiring, promotion, and other occupational and educational opportunities, many people who recognize their own depression will not seek treatment because of concerns that they may have to report it later.

Symptoms of Depression

There is no blood test for depression. The diagnosis is based on the reports of sufferers about how they feel and on observations of how they look and behave made by doctors and by people who know them well.

> John D. was a forty-five-year-old, self-employed, successful businessman when he suddenly initiated negotiations to sell his company. For months preceding the decision to sell, John had experienced increasing fatigue and decreasing ability to concentrate, which he attributed to the pressures of work. He quit meeting his friends for golf on Sunday afternoons, preferring to sleep in front of the television, but then had problems going to sleep at night. John's appetite, energy level, and sex drive gradually diminished, while he experienced a growing sense of restlessness, irritability, and futility. John's wife became concerned when she learned of her husband's recent purchase of additional life insurance and of his revision of his will. She convinced John to see his family physician for a "good physical."

The symptoms of depression fall into four categories: mood, cognitive, behavioral, and physical. In other words, depression affects how individuals feel, think, and behave as well as how their bodies work. People with depression may experience symptoms in any or all of the categories, depending on personal characteristics and the severity and type of depression.

Depressed people generally describe their mood as sad, depressed, anxious, or flat. Victims of depression often report additional feelings of emptiness, hopelessness, pessimism, uselessness, worthlessness, helplessness, unreasonable guilt, and profound apathy. Their self-esteem is usually low, and they may feel overwhelmed, restless, or irritable. Loss of interest in activities previously enjoyed is common and is usually accompanied by a diminished ability to feel pleasure, even in sexual activity.

As the illness worsens, the cognitive ability of the brain is affected. Slowed thinking, difficulty with concentration, memory lapses, and problems with decision-making become obvious. Those losses lead to frustration and further aggravate the person's mounting sense of being overwhelmed. The sufferer longs for escape, and thoughts of death intrude, sometimes taking the form of wishful thinking, as in "I wish God would just take me" or "I wish I could vanish," and often involving ideas of suicide.

In its most severe forms, depression causes major abnormalities in the way sufferers see the world around them. They may become psychotic, believing things that are not true or seeing and hearing imaginary people or objects.

> Ann H. was forty years old when her husband took her to the family physician after she began crying daily and begging her husband to take good care of their teenage daughters after her death. Despite a normal medical assessment, Ann remained convinced that she was dying of metastatic cancer as had her mother years before. She "felt" the cancer cells destroying her liver and kidneys and pointed to her twenty-pound weight loss in six months as proof of terminal illness. Ann's appetite was poor, yet she remained constantly, unproductively active throughout the day. At night she lay awake crying about leaving her daughters without a mother, while during the day she worried constantly about becoming an emotional and financial burden on her family in the late stages of her "terminal" illness. Ann decided she must kill herself to protect her family and took a lethal overdose of an antidepressant medication that had been prescribed by her family physician.

Psychosis in depression is not rare. Between 10 and 25 percent of patients hospitalized for serious depression, especially elderly patients, develop psychotic symptoms. Symptoms of psychosis may include delusions (irrational beliefs that cannot be resolved with rational explanations) and hallucinations (seeing, hearing, feeling, tasting, or smelling things or people that are not present).

People with psychoses may develop paranoia, believing that they are being manipulated by known or unknown people or forces, that there is a conspiracy against them, or that they are in danger. No amount of rational explanation changes the delusional belief. Others may be convinced that they have committed an unpardonable sin against loved ones or against their God and deserve severe punishment, even death. Some sufferers become so firmly convinced of their own worthlessness that they begin to view themselves as a burden to their families and choose to kill themselves. Occasionally, severe depression may result in hallucinations in which the depressed person hears or sees things or people that are not present; other types of hallucinations, such as smelling or feeling things that are not present, are less common in severe depression than in some other brain disorders.

The changes occurring with depression understandably result in alterations in behavior. Most individuals with moderate-to-severe depression will experience decreased activity levels and appear withdrawn and less talkative, although some severely depressed individuals show agitation and restless behavior, such as pacing the floor, wringing their hands, and gripping and massaging their foreheads. Given a choice, most begin to avoid people and activities, yet others will be most uncomfortable when alone or not distracted. In general, the severely depressed become less productive, although they may successfully mask the decline in performance if they have been highly productive in the past. In the workplace, depression may result in morale problems, absenteeism, decreased productivity, increased accidents, frequent complaints of fatigue, references to unexplained aches and pains, and alcohol and drug abuse. Severely depressed individuals have been known to work their regular schedule during the day, interact with their coworkers in a routine way, and then go home and kill themselves.

Depression is more than a mental illness. It is a total body illness. People suffering from moderate-to-severe depression experience changes in their body functions. Their energy levels fall, and they fatigue more easily. Insomnia is common and takes many forms; depressed individuals may have difficulty going to sleep or experience early morning awakenings. A subgroup of depressed patients feel an excessive need for sleep. Depressives consistently complain that their sleep is not restful and that they feel just as tired in the morning when they awake as they did when they went to bed the evening before. Some may be troubled by dreams that carry the depressive tone into sleeping hours, causing abrupt awakenings due to distress.

Appetite changes are common. Most depressives experience decreased or total loss of appetite, with associated weight loss resulting in lower energy levels. The same individuals who oversleep when depressed also tend to overeat. They gain weight from a combination of increased caloric intake and decreased activity level, which compounds their problems through increased frustration and lowered self-esteem. Whether the appetite increases or decreases, the end result is a vicious cycle of physical symptoms aggravating the depression.

Physical complaints are common and may or may not have a physical basis. Many seriously depressed people, in fact, first go to their physicians with physical complaints. The depressed mood may not be recognized initially by these patients, especially if they are men. Men, in general, are less apt to look inward when they "feel bad," attempting instead to locate the problem in their environment.

Physical symptoms associated with depression can occur in any part of the body and can include pain (headache, backache), gastrointestinal problems (nausea, stomach pain, diarrhea, constipation), neurologic complaints (dizziness, numbness, memory problems), sexual disorders (lack of desire, failure of orgasm), and general complaints of feeling unwell and heavy, as if one's feet are stuck in mud. The physical complaints of depressed patients cannot be overlooked, because many studies indicate an increased risk of real physical illness in people who have severe forms of depression. The reasons for this are unclear, but will be further discussed in chapter 2.

Depression and Suicide

Every 17.3 minutes someone commits suicide in the United States. According to National Institute of Mental Health statistics, suicide is the ninth leading cause of death in Americans and accounts for more than 30,000 deaths every year. More Americans die of suicide than are victims of homicide. Although most people who become depressed do not commit suicide, depression can be a lethal illness. Contrary to popular belief, not everyone who commits suicide is depressed, but the majority of people who commit suicide do so during a severe depressive episode. The suicide risk in people with severe depression ranges between 15 and 30 percent, with approximately seven suicide attempts for every successful suicide. Women are two to three times more likely to attempt suicide, but men are four to five times more likely to be successful in their attempt.

Over 70 percent of all suicides in the United States are committed by white men, and the majority of those deaths involve firearms. The second highest rate in the country is reported in white women, followed by rates for black women. Black men in the United States currently have the lowest suicide rate; unfortunately, it is rising.

> Bob T. was a seventy-two-year-old retired government employee who lived alone in a retirement community. He had been the sole caretaker for his wife, who had been bedridden for two years before her death the previous year. Bob was hypertensive and diabetic. Both conditions had been well controlled with diet and medication until the past few months. Despite repeated visits to his physician, Bob did not feel well. He experienced vague stomach discomfort, joint aches, increasing insomnia, and fatigue, which he reported to his doctor on repeated visits. Bob did not discuss with his physician his fear that his memory was failing rapidly and that he might have "old-timer's disease." He often thought of his wife in a "happier place" and longed to join her. One Sunday afternoon after attending church services, Bob

went home, wrote his name and the current date in the family Bible below the entry noting his wife's death, and shot himself in the head.

Thoughts of suicide may be intermittent and relatively brief, but they may also be persistent and intrusive, developing into plans for carrying it out. Circumstances that increase the risk for suicide in depressed patients include advancing age, male sex, Caucasian race, living alone, chronic medical illness, a recent major loss, substance abuse, panic attacks, psychotic symptoms, previous episodes of depression, previous suicide attempts, and family history of depression. In addition, people who are depressed and simultaneously have other brain disorders such as schizophrenia, dementia, or brain damage from illness or trauma may be at increased risk for suicide because of impaired judgment and a tendency toward impulsiveness.

Common methods of suicide include gunshot wound to the head or chest, overdose of over-the-counter or prescription medications, overdose of street drugs, laceration of neck or wrists with a sharp object such as a razor blade or a knife or broken glass, asphyxiation by hanging or from the breathing of a toxic gas such as natural gas or carbon monoxide from an automobile exhaust, and purposeful "accidents," such as car crashes against trees or off bridges. In the past, women were reported to choose less violent means of suicide, such as overdose or asphyxiation by gas, while men chose more violent means, such as guns. Now, however, suicide by firearms is the most common method for both men and women, accounting for over half of all suicides. Unfortunately, depressed people intent on suicide can be very creative in choosing their method of death, despite the efforts of their doctors and their loved ones to prevent the tragedy.

The risk for suicide, ironically, may be greatest when the sufferers have passed the lowest point in the course of their illness and have begun to recover. The reasons are not clear but may relate to the observation that recovery from depression often begins with an increase in energy level without immediate improvement in mood. When such is the case, depressed people in the early stages of recovery have regained enough energy to plan and carry out a long-desired suicide. It may also be that once seriously depressed individuals finally make the decision to escape the anguish of illness through death, they feel a temporary reprieve from their symptoms.

Suicide may occur without warning, but 80 percent of people who attempt or commit suicide do give some indication of their intent by means such as voicing despair and world-weariness, expressing suicidal thoughts, threatening to harm themselves, increasing the use of alcohol or drugs, or writing suicide notes. Rehearsing suicide or seriously discussing specific methods may also indicate a determination to go forward with it. More often the hints are subtle behavioral changes that may serve as red flags. Such warnings perhaps indicating that the despondent individual is putting his or her house in order may include making out a will, reviewing life insurance coverage, purchasing cemetery plots, giving away valued possessions, or getting in touch with close relatives. Contrary to popular understanding, most people do not leave notes.

Once someone has decided to commit suicide, it may be impossible to prevent the tragedy. Although many suicide attempters are ambivalent about their course of action until the last moment, others are determined to die and give few clues ahead of time.

Types of Depression

Many different and sometimes complicated systems attempt to classify depressions according to their symptoms, severity, causes, and other characteristics. One reason for these rigorous attempts is the need to conduct research on relatively pure forms of the illness. Such research should result in improved treatment for the various forms of depression.

The two most common systems use similar terms in naming various types of depression. The international version is the ninth edition of the *International Classification of Diseases*, commonly referred to as *ICD-9*, which classifies all medical and mental disorders. The system used by most clinicians in the United States is the *Diagnostic and Statistical Manual of Mental Disorders*, fourth edition, or *DSM-IV*, produced by the American Psychiatric Association. Further attempts are made to standardize these common classification systems with each new edition.

Depression can take many forms, and these may be of varying degrees of severity with different natural courses. The types of depression commonly diagnosed in the United States include adjustment disorder with depressed mood; dysthymic disorder; major depressive disorder, single episode or recurrent; major depressive episode associated with bipolar disorder; and mood disorder associated with a general medical condition.

Mild mood alterations do not require help and therefore are not matters for diagnosis. For instance, a bad mood is just that— temporary frustration associated with current circumstances. A person exhibiting a somewhat more persistent alteration of mood is often described as being "blue," "bummed out," or mildly depressed. People with such negative feelings still enjoy their hobbies, family, and friends. Such mild depressions are usually time-limited and unlikely to require treatment.

Moderate-to-severe forms of depression frequently come to the attention of caregivers, although the initial complaint may not be depression. Those are the forms of depression that fall into formal diagnostic categories.

Bereavement

Bereavement, or grief, is a normal feeling of sadness that occurs following the loss of a loved one. Uncomplicated grief is believed to advance through a series of stages that, in many aspects, mimic the illness depression, raising questions as to where normal bereavement ends and major depressive illness begins. The initial stage of grief occurs during the first few weeks after the loss and is experienced as feelings of disbelief and shock. It is commonly associated with bouts of crying, loss of appetite, loss of sexual drive, restless sleep or insomnia, lack of energy, and difficulty concentrating. In women, disturbances in the menstrual cycle are common.

The intermediate stage of grief takes place during the first year after the death of the loved one. During that phase, feelings of intense loneliness and sadness are accompanied by persistent thoughts about the death, the events leading up to the death, why it happened, and how it could have been prevented. Limited capacity for pleasure, lack of energy, sleep and appetite problems, and bouts of tearfulness persist to varying degrees.

The recovery phase of grief is the time when people begin to return to their social lives and "get on with life." That usually begins about the second year following the loss.

Little is known about the actual duration of normal grief. Studies of spouses and parents dealing with unexpected loss point to normal grief processes lasting up to seven years. Sudden death often causes bouts of grief that are more severe and longer lasting than the bereavement following an anticipated death.

Death of a spouse can have significant impact on the health of the surviving partner. Women tend to be at increased risk for health problems within the first three months after the loss. Men whose spouses die are particularly likely to develop emotional or physical problems during the first year after the loss and have an increased mortality rate. Bereaved men who remarry tend to have lower mortality rates than those who do not.

Death of a child is particularly likely to produce severe grief reactions regardless of the age of the parent and child. Bereaved parents experience high levels of psychological distress that are accompanied by changes in physical health, functional activities, and family cohesion, including an increased risk of divorce.

The distinction between "normal" grief and depression can be a difficult one to make. The two states share many similar physical and emotional symptoms, and the duration of both can be prolonged. Grief can produce a preoccupation with guilt about actions taken or not taken surrounding the death of a loved one and thoughts that the survivor would be better off dead. Experiences of transiently hearing or seeing the deceased loved one can also be a part of the normal grief process, especially in some cultures. Morbid rumination regarding other feelings of guilt, a sense of worthlessness, anticipated death of other loved ones, prolonged decrease in level of function, marked slowness of behavior or speech, reports of unusual beliefs, or persistent or recurring hallucinations should be considered outside the normal grief process and more indicative of a major depressive episode. When symptoms of severe grief extend more than two months beyond the death of a loved one, treatment with antidepressant medication may be needed in addition to supportive psychotherapy.

Grief in young children is most profound when it involves the death of a parent or a primary caretaker. It can produce such behaviors as crying, calling and searching for the deceased loved one, and refusing to be comforted. Emotional withdrawal often occurs and is associated with sad facial expressions, lethargy, and lack of interest in former activities. Eating and sleeping may be disrupted. Children may regress by losing some of their developmental milestones; i.e., toilet-trained toddlers may begin to soil themselves again. Bereaved young children may become detached and lack much facial expression. They often are very sensitive to any reminder of the lost loved one. Grief in young children is generally treated with supportive measures; use of antidepressant medication is usually not required.

Adjustment Disorder with Depression

Adjustment disorder with depression is the term for the condition commonly referred to as situational depression or reactive depression. Individuals with this malady feel sadness about a loss or a major life change. The sadness, depressed mood, or sense of hopelessness begins within three months of a major stress and is excessive. People with this form of depression may find it difficult to carry on routine activities at home, at work, or at school. The depression gradually disappears once the stress is over and is not usually considered a serious depression, although it may be very uncomfortable. Often the support and advice of concerned friends, loved ones, or a doctor are enough to help sufferers manage until their mood improves following removal of stress or a decrease in its intensity.

Dysthymic Disorder

Some depressions are chronic and can last a lifetime. Dysthymic disorder, or dysthymia, describes a more chronic condition in which individuals experience depression for most of the day, most of the time, for at least two years. Brief periods of relatively normal mood may intervene, but those periods of relief last no more than a couple of months at a time. Depression of this type may last for years, even a lifetime. Dysthymic disorder is chronic but not usually severe, yet it may cause significant problems in everyday life.

Major Depressive Disorder

Major depressive disorder (also known as unipolar depression or clinical depression) is the serious and often disabling form of depression that can occur as a single episode or as a series of depressive episodes over a lifetime. The course of major depressive disorder is variable. A single episode may last as little as two weeks or as long as months to years. Some people will have only one episode with full recovery. Others recover from the initial episode only to experience another one months to years later. There may be clusters of episodes followed by years of remission. Some individuals have increasingly frequent depressive episodes as they grow older.

During major depressive episodes, sufferers will have most, if not all, of the depressive symptoms affecting the mood, cognitive, behavioral, and physical aspects of life. The most severe forms of major depressive disorder may result in delusions and the other psychotic abnormalities described earlier in this chapter. This is one of the most disabling forms of depression.

Bipolar Disorder

Bipolar disorder is a so-called "mood swing disorder" formerly known by the more familiar term "manic-depressive illness." This disorder has been described in ancient texts around the world and has been the subject of focused research since the 1800s because of its tendency toward dramatic presentations and because of the challenging management problems associated with it.

Bipolar disorder is classified based on the severity of the episodic mood elevations that are interspersed with major depressive episodes. In addition to episodes of severe depression, people with bipolar disorder type I experience at least one episode of mania—that is, an episode during which their mood ranges unpredictably from euphoric to irritable and is accompanied by hyperactivity, lack of need for sleep, impulsiveness, rapid thoughts and speech, poor follow-through in tasks, poor judgment in business and personal arenas, poor insight (self-awareness of changes in attitude and behavior), delusions of wealth or power or victimization by conspiracies, and often, but not always, auditory hallucinations. Visual hallucinations occur in mania, but are not as common as auditory hallucinations. Manic episodes can last for a few hours or for months, but generally extend for days to a few weeks. Manic episodes usually do not last as long as the depressive episodes also associated with this disorder. Taken as a group, bipolars tend to experience manic episodes more frequently in their young adult years than later in the course of their illness, when depressive episodes are likely to predominate. Many bipolar patients are reluctant to give up their manic episodes, even though they want relief from the depressive ones. For that reason, they often will not take mood stabilizing medications as required. Patients are at risk for suicide attempts during both manic and depressive episodes, especially when the manic symptoms become so intense as to cause agitation and psychotic symptoms.

People with bipolar disorder type II show a similar pattern of recurrent depressions punctuated by occasional mood elevations, except that the mood elevation is milder and is described as hypomania. Individuals with hypomania tend to experience episodically expansive but controllable "highs" and increased productivity while retaining reasonable insight and judgment. These "little highs" may last only a few hours before a mood swing occurs and increasingly severe depressive symptoms set in. Still, bipolar type II patients enjoy their natural highs and are loath to give them up.

Recently clinicians have become more aware of other variations of bipolar disorder often referred to as atypical bipolar disorders. Those disorders include bipolar disorder with mixed mood and rapid cycling bipolar disorder. The former is a variant in which the patient experiences episodes that appear to be a combination of the worst features of both mania and depression. The patient may be hyperactive, with rapid speech, racing thoughts, erratic behavior, agitation, and poor judgment typical of mania but at the same time report feelings of intense depression and hopelessness and thoughts of suicide. Clinical experience indicates that this can be a lethal combination.

Rapid cyclers are individuals with bipolar disorder who experience four or more significant mood swings per year. As this group has been more closely studied over the last decade, researchers and clinicians have identified individuals who cycle as frequently as weekly, daily, and even many times in a single day. Needless to say, people with ultrarapid cycling (ultradians, as they are sometimes called) are a miserable lot, searching desperately for answers and effective treatment while hampered by emotional overload. One such ultradian patient described herself as experiencing a "continuous mental El Niño."

Atypical Mood Disorders

Mood disorders do not always cooperate by appearing as pure, clear-cut diagnostic entities. Sometimes the presentation of the illness is so complicated that diagnosis and treatment become an exercise in detective work. The most common of the atypical presentations includes a curious, episodic mood swing disorder associated with seasonal changes, a condition known as seasonal affective disorder, or SAD. This condition, which will be discussed more thoroughly in later chapters, usually involves annual autumn/winter depressive episodes that clear in the late spring and summer.

Seasonal mood swings can be manic rather than depressive. In late summer of each year, psychiatrists commonly anticipate significant increases in the hospital admission of patients with acute mania; hence the insiders' instruction for neophyte psychiatrists that "manics run in August." Is this phenomenon related to SAD, or is it simply a variant of bipolar disorder? Perhaps SAD is part of a spectrum disorder with major depressive disorder on one end and bipolar disorder on the other.

In another atypical and complex mood disorder called double depression, sufferers experience a chronic low-grade depression (dysthymia) periodically intensified by episodes of major depression. This disorder can be difficult to diagnose initially, but becomes more apparent after antidepressant medication trials provide relief from the more incapacitating depressive symptoms but leave chronic, low-grade mood symptoms that do not improve with continued medication changes. At that point the clinician may suspect the presence of two simultaneously occurring depressive disorders. To further complicate the picture, clinical experience indicates that atypical depressions are often accompanied by other chronic psychiatric manifestations such as anxiety and obsessive-compulsive symptoms.

Mood Disorder Associated with General Medical Condition

Depressive symptoms are common in medical and surgical patients and are formally diagnosed as depression with general medical condition where the specific medical condition is named. The reasons are varied and complex, but common issues include loss of health, helplessness, lowered self-esteem, fear for the future, feelings of vulnerability, chronic disability and pain, financial stresses, and alterations in personal relationships. While depression may be secondary to the stresses of medical or surgical illness, it may also be a result of medications used to treat those conditions. For instance, many of the current medicines used to treat hypertension have a well-known tendency to cause or to aggravate depression.

While patients whose depression is associated with medical or surgical illnesses often do not meet the criteria for major depressive disorder, they do have many of the same total body symptoms. Their mood, however, appears to be related to their medical situation and tends to improve or resolve when the medical or surgical condition is stabilized. One difficulty with this diagnosis is that many of the physical illnesses that affect the human body (such as thyroid disease, diabetes, cancer of the pancreas, and chronic heart disease) may produce symptoms similar to those seen in depression, yet the treatment of choice may be simply to treat the medical illness. If the depressive symptoms do not go away with improvement in the medical or surgical condition, the patient may be suffering from a major depressive disorder.

Depression lasting two years or more is generally one of three types: (1) chronic major depressive disorder, (2) dysthymic disorder, or (3) double depression.

A common misconception regarding serious depressive episodes is that depression represents a normal response to the stresses faced by individuals. Whether or not an identifiable stress appears to have precipitated a serious depression, depression once started often has a life of its own, independent of the stress. The disabling effects of depression should not be minimized and should be treated aggressively.

2. Who Gets Depressed?

"I used to think that only weak people got depressed. Now I guess I'm one of the weak ones."

—A man in midlife

Twenty percent of the world's population is at risk for depression at some time in their lives, and one might assume that such a common illness would be easily recognized. This, unfortunately, is not the case. Depression is a great illusionist, skillfully misdirecting with sleight of hand so that unwary people look in the wrong direction for answers to the puzzle of their misery. The cluster of symptoms fed by depression may trigger concerns regarding a person's physical health, the stability of close relationships or work situations, and even the value of self, without disclosing the true culprit.

The symptoms of depression vary with the severity and form of the disorder and often with the circumstances of onset. Often depression looks like the "garden variety" mood disorder we recognize. The sufferers feel depressed, look depressed, and act depressed. They experience predictable changes in sleep, appetite, energy level, activity level, concentration, and outlook on life. This straightforward presentation of depression can occur at any stage in the life cycle.

At times depression appears in disguised forms. That is particularly true of depressions occurring in special segments of the population, such as children, teenagers, postpartum mothers, "midlifers," the elderly, or people with serious medical illnesses.

The first episode of major depression usually occurs in a person's twenties, with the rate of depression peaking between ages fifty-five to seventy years in men and thirty-five to forty-five years in women. Although about 20 percent of depressions last two years or more, the average duration of the illness is eight months. In 40 percent of cases there is only one episode, but in half the depression returns within two years. People who have repeated episodes of depression on the average will experience about seven episodes in a lifetime. In some, the depressive episodes begin abruptly and recovery is total, while others have a slower onset and a less complete recovery. Treatment with antidepressant medications or electroconvulsive therapy can reduce episodes to an average of four months.

Depression in Children

We tend to think of childhood as a happy, carefree time filled with summer vacations, chocolate sundaes, soccer, and weekend morning cartoons on television. Perhaps that is the scenario for many children in the United States. Tragically, it is not the case for all.

Mark W. was an eleven-year-old boy who lived with his parents, both working professionals, and his eight-year-old sister in an upscale suburban community. Mark had always been an obedient child and a good student, so his parents were surprised to receive a note from one of his teachers requesting a parent-teacher conference. During the conference, Mr. and Mrs. W. discovered that Mark had been skipping classes, failing to complete homework assignments, performing poorly on math and science quizzes, and returning his report cards unsigned. The teacher noted that Mark seemed irritable and had begun picking fights with classmates at recess. He was disrespectful to teachers and disruptive in class. When she confronted the boy with his behavior, he burst into tears and ran from the room.

Children are at particular risk for underdiagnosis and undertreatment of depression. Most of us intuitively understand that children living in distressing circumstances, such as those involving parental abuse or neglect, can develop emotional problems that look like depression—lethargy, apathy, and withdrawal. We fail to recognize, however, that children may experience depressive symptoms in less obvious situations. For instance, children under four years of age can develop behaviors reminiscent of depression when separated from their parents for even a few days.

Periodic moodiness is common in children, but as many as 2.5 percent of young children may experience prolonged and persistent episodes of depression. The recognition of depression in children is complicated by the fact that in them the illness may not look like the adult variety. Children are particularly prone to experience depression in association with behavior or anxiety disorders.

Some children do experience the classical depressive symptoms: sadness, withdrawal including avoidance of friends and refusal to attend school, apathy, low energy level, poor appetite, excessive sleeping, multiple physical complaints, and school performance problems indicative of concentration difficulties.

Other children fall victim to the great illusionist, with patterns of behavior that mislead concerned adults. Children may be unable to articulate their sadness, complaining instead of boredom or inability to have fun. They may cry, be brutally self-critical, and think about death. Others may become overactive, argumentative, and impulsive rather than lethargic, appear irritable rather than sad, and engage in behaviors more reminiscent of delinquency than of mood disorder. Some children who develop serious conduct problems experience a major depression (recognized only in retrospect) immediately preceding the development of the severe behavior problems.

Depression in childhood is often recurrent and persistent and is potentially serious. It affects boys and girls equally, although by adolescence more girls are stricken than boys. There is evidence that children of parents who have experienced serious depression are at increased risk for developing serious depressions themselves with significant impairment before the age of twenty. That observation was reinforced by a 1997 study of 182 children from 91 families in which one or both parents suffered from mood disorders. The study, conducted by Myrna M. Weissman and her associates, concluded that children of depressed parents are a high-risk group for onset of anxiety disorders and major depressive disorders in childhood as well as major depressive disorders and alcohol dependence in adolescence and early adulthood. The study supported the potential value of early detection in the offspring of depressed parents.

Although childhood depression is strongly familial, episodes of depression can be triggered by emotionally traumatic losses such as the death of a parent or sibling, parental divorce, serious illness, or a move to a new neighborhood or school, especially under trying circumstances.

Most prepubertal children with depression will recover within two years, but almost three-quarters of them will have another episode within five years. Those whose depressions last longer have a poorer outcome even when the depression is milder. Older depressed children may be prone to more severe and longer-lasting depressions than younger depressed children.

Depression in Teenagers and Young People

Depression in teenagers and young people is also seriously underdiagnosed. Approximately 4 percent of teenagers suffer severe depression each year.

Kristin S. was a sixteen-year-old high school student who lived with her parents and two younger brothers in a small town in the Midwest. Popular and a good student, she was active in organized extracurricular events in the community until the spring of her junior year, when she declined to try out for the varsity cheerleading team and dropped out of the school band. She began spending long hours alone in her room listening to rock music, writing morbid poetry, and reading from a volume of poems by Edgar Allen Poe, memorizing her favorites—"The Raven" and "Annabel Lee." Although she maintained her grades, Kristin often fell asleep in class. She began avoiding activities with her friends and curtailed phone visits with them. When approached by her concerned mother, Kristin remarked that her friends were "silly" and that she was tired of doing what everyone else wanted her to do.

Many behaviors considered normal in teenagers, such as increased sleeping, decreased interaction with family members, gloomy introspection, and heightened sensitivity, may sometimes be part of a depressive syndrome. Depression in teenagers can lead to problems in school performance, decreased productivity at work, damaged relationships with family and with friends, legal problems, and suicide.

Depressed teens may experience the same symptoms as depressed adults. Variations in teenage depression, however, may require a shrewd observer. Instead of voicing sadness, teenagers may write poetry with morbid themes, be drawn to nihilistic literature or music, or wear black clothes. Their grades may fall as a result of difficulties with concentration and sluggish thinking. Sleep disturbance may be demonstrated by all-night television watching, difficulty getting up in the morning, or going to sleep during classes. They may complain of pervasive boredom rather than depression. Depressed teenagers show increased moodiness and irritability as well as a tendency to be self-critical. They may be constantly angry, becoming argumentative and rebellious. They experience difficulties with concentration, changes in sleep and appetite patterns, loss of energy, lack of interest in usual activities and friends, and feelings of despair and emptiness. They may talk of death and dying, drift into alcohol or drug abuse, and threaten suicide.

Each year in the United States, almost five thousand young people between the ages of fifteen and twenty-four kill themselves. The suicide rate for this group has nearly tripled since 1960, making it the third leading cause of death in teenagers (exceeded only by accidents and homicides) and the second leading cause of death in college-age youths.

Suicide attempts in teenagers usually follow an acute crisis in association with more chronic problems. The crisis may appear insignificant to parents and other adults, but to the teenager the situation is distressing and seems permanent. Common precipitants for suicide attempts in teenagers include loss of a boyfriend or girlfriend, a crush on an unattainable person, academic problems, a family argument, or fear of embarrassment.

Teenagers who experience their parents' divorce, a disruptive family, physical or sexual abuse, alcohol or substance abuse, or the suicide of a relative or close friend are at increased risk for suicide attempts. Many more teenagers attempt suicide than actually succeed. This may be due in part to the fact that they are often naïve in their choice of methods. Unsuccessful attempts in teenagers, unfortunately, are often misinterpreted as being manipulative. All suicide attempts, especially those in teenagers, should be taken seriously and considered a cry for help.

Depression in Women

We have known for centuries that women are more prone to depression than are men. Some forms of depression are at least twice as common in women. In fact, 25 percent of women are likely to experience a severe depression at some time in their lives, yet only about one-fifth will receive the treatment they need.

Before puberty, the risk of depression is about equal for boys and girls. Beginning at puberty, however, females experience a greater risk for depression than do males, and the difference in the risk rates becomes more pronounced between the ages of eighteen and forty-four years. According to the National Mental Health Association, the sex difference in depression rates is less pronounced between the ages of forty-four and sixty-five years, but after age sixty-five, women are again much more likely than men to develop severe depression.

The pattern of symptoms and individual responses to depressive illness also varies according to sex. When men become depressed, they tend to look outside themselves for the cause and take action to "correct" or master their environment. They search for distraction in the form of increased physical activities, recreation with friends, and work-related projects. Such endeavors serve to give men a sense of mastery and control over the external conditions that they believe responsible for their discomfort.

Depressed women, on the other hand, are prone to search within themselves for the source of their unhappiness, brooding and dwelling on their problems. They experience associated anxiety, sleep problems, panic attacks, and eating disorders more frequently than do depressed men. They often feel out of control and helpless to meet life's expectations, while blaming themselves for being unable to face their responsibilities.

The reasons for the sex differences in severe depression have been debated for decades. Proposed causes have included hormonal, interpersonal, and power issues.

After puberty, under the influence of their complex hormonal systems, many women experience monthly mood shifts. Although these are usually relatively mild episodes of moodiness and irritability lasting only a day or so, premenstrual depression can be severe in some women. Women commonly report episodes of depression associated with other major hormone changes in their life cycle—i.e., while on birth control pills, following childbirth, and during menopause.

Most physicians believe that depression provoked by use of birth control pills is relatively uncommon, especially with the newer oral contraceptives. Many women disagree. Mood alterations in women on birth control pills may not be reported to physicians because the changes are often subtle and gradual in onset. They may take the form of moodiness or irritability, which the women generally attempt to ignore, although their partners and other family members may have greater difficulty doing so.

> After a three-year courtship, Melissa V. began taking oral contraceptives two months before her planned wedding and continued the birth control pills for over a year without recognizing any difficulties with the medication other than periodic nausea, increased frequency of headaches, and weight gain. When the couple were ready to start their family, the young woman discontinued the contraceptives, became pregnant, and delivered a healthy infant whom she breast-fed. Once the baby was weaned, Melissa prepared to resume taking the birth control pills, but her husband suggested they use alternative means of contraception. He confided to her that he had noticed mood and personality changes in her within a few weeks after she had begun taking the birth control pills, although he had not made the association between the two events until she discontinued the pills in preparation for starting a family, at which point she returned to her formal cheerful and less irritable self.

Menopause is a time in women's lives when their estrogen and progesterone cycles begin to fluctuate erratically until ovarian production of those hormones largely ceases. Physicians and women have tended to relate depressive disorders that occur during menopause to hormonal irregularities or deficiencies. An association between the decreasing ovarian hormone production and onset of depression has not yet been scientifically confirmed. Although estrogen supplementation during and after menopause may help prevent mild forms of depression, estrogen alone is not an effective treatment for moderate-to-severe depression. Ironically, the progesterone often prescribed along with estrogen to menopausal women in an effort to "normalize" their hormonal status may be associated with worsening of mood.

Clinicians who study people and their relationships note that women tend to place greater value on personal relationships than do men. It is speculated that the greater need for emotional connectedness demonstrated by women may place them in a more vulnerable position with regard to mood stability, because the success of relationships cannot be determined by one person alone.

Since the time of Freud, the power status of women relative to men has been discussed as a contributor to emotional symptoms in women. Many women do experience feelings of low self-esteem and self-worth resulting partly from cultural factors. As a rule, girls are less likely to receive encouragement to be active in team sports where productive competitiveness and self-reliance are learned. Women whose cultures tend to value "masculine" traits over "feminine" traits and to limit educational and employment opportunities for women outside the home are thought by some experts to be at greater risk for undiagnosed and therefore untreated depression. Other experts disagree, charging that this conclusion is an erroneous product of Western values and biased against those cultures that "shelter" their women.

There is evidence that in Western culture marriage seems to provide a protective effect for men but is a stressor for women. Contrary to popular opinion, studies tend to show that married women experience more depression than do single women. The National Mental Health Association reports that depression is more common among women who stay home full-time with their small children than among women in the general population.

Although depressed women benefit from antidepressant medications, they tend to receive relatively less benefit than do men and to experience greater levels of side effects. That may be due to physical differences in the way men's and women's bodies handle medications. Hormone shifts are an obvious example. Another significant difference is women's relatively greater fat deposits, which soak up and store antidepressants, making less medication initially available in the bloodstream for delivery to the brain. Gastrointestinal differences between men and women also affect the way in which the stomach and intestines absorb medications.

Depression in Women Following Childbirth

Many women experience some mood changes after childbirth. The mild form of mood alteration experienced by two-thirds of mothers following the birth of a child is commonly known as postpartum blues. This is a mild, transient change in mood which usually begins within one to five days following delivery, lasts a few days to a couple of weeks, and does not require treatment. Mothers of newborns typically experience sadness or rapidly changing moods, bouts of crying without clear cause, appetite changes, and insomnia or excessive drowsiness. A mother in such a situation usually recognizes that her behavior is out of proportion to the situation but is at a loss to explain it unless someone (usually another mother) has prepared her ahead of time for this curious phenomenon. Following the birth of her first child, one physician-mother was watching Apaches and the U.S. Cavalry assault each other in an old western movie on television and found herself bursting into tears because all those mothers' sons were being killed on both sides of the battle. Luckily another woman had told her about the postpartum blues so that she did not think she had lost her mind.

The cause of postpartum blues is still not known. Experts vary in attributing the cause either to abrupt hormonal changes following childbirth or to the sudden and constant increase in responsibility or to a combination of both.

True depression is different from postpartum blues. The potentially severe depression that can occur following both childbirth and unsuccessful pregnancies, including spontaneous and voluntary abortions, is known as postpartum depression. Women may have difficulty in distinguishing where postpartum blues end and postpartum depression begins, because new mothers are often sleep-deprived, fatigued, and preoccupied with the constant care of their newborn and may not initially note the progression of their symptoms from mild to severe.

> Jane D., a twenty-four-year-old woman, was hospitalized for psychiatric care following the murder of her infant son. At the time of her admission to the hospital, Jane did not understand that her child was dead. As a result of her advanced pregnancy, Jane had quit her job and moved to a rural area to live with her baby's father and his parents. The blended family got along well. Jane had an uneventful pregnancy and delivered a healthy baby boy. She did well following delivery and was a devoted mother until the baby was two months old, when she began staying awake all night to check on her son every few minutes. She became moody, tearful, and wary of other members of the household. She refused to eat food prepared for her and limited her dietary intake to liquids and foods available in sealed containers. Jane ceased talking to the family and sat for hours holding her baby and mumbling under her breath. One afternoon the baby's father and grandfather went into the backyard with hoes and shovels to prepare the garden for planting. When Jane saw them digging a hole, she became despondent, fearful that the men were going to kill her child and bury it there. She rushed to the kitchen, grabbed a knife, and stabbed the infant in order to "protect the baby from being murdered" by its father.

Postpartum depression is a serious illness that can threaten the lives of both the mother and her newborn. It is not a rare disorder, occurring in almost 15 percent of women. Women who experience one episode of postpartum depression are likely to suffer recurrences following subsequent pregnancies. This serious depressive illness when untreated can persist for months and may be associated with psychotic symptoms.

As with postpartum blues, the cause of postpartum depression is not known. Factors that seem to be associated with the disorder include abrupt hormone changes following childbirth, fatigue associated with long days and nights of newborn care, a sense of letdown following a period of excitement, the realization of profound changes in lifestyle, and a sense of isolation. Postpartum depression does not result from someone's having a character flaw or being poor motherhood material.

Postpartum depression can be divided into two types based on time of onset of the major symptoms. Early-onset postpartum depression, which may seem like postpartum blues, begins within the first few days or weeks after birth. It is generally a milder form of the disorder and may not require extensive treatment.

Late-onset postpartum depression appears several weeks after the birth, and involves the insidious development of feelings of intense sadness, depression, chronic fatigue, lack of energy, inability to sleep, appetite and weight changes, loss of sexual drive, difficulty in concentrating, and, occasionally, physical symptoms such as hair loss. Delusions, hallucinations, suicidal thoughts, and homicidal thoughts (toward the newborn and other children) can occur in the most severe cases. Homicidal thoughts toward children may be based on a psychotic notion of protecting them from the dangers of life, especially if the mother is contemplating suicide and believes that she will not be around.

Postpartum mania can occur within the same time frame as postpartum depression. This usually occurs in women who later experience a severe depressive episode and are finally diagnosed with bipolar disorder.

Considering the frequency of depression following childbirth and the controversy in the United States surrounding elective abortion, we might expect that women who undergo such abortions would suffer a high incidence of depression afterward. Research to date has not found that to be the case.

Depression in Fathers Following the Birth of a Child

Although most discussions of postpartum depression center on mothers, fathers of newborns can also experience postpartum letdowns. Fathers presumably do not have abrupt hormonal and physiological changes after the birth of their children. They do, however, experience adjustment problems due to increased responsibilities, sudden lifestyle changes resulting from the addition of an infant to the family fold, and increased financial burdens. Feelings of isolation often occur in a man as the woman who has heretofore been his lover becomes intensely focused on her infant and neglects the emotional and sexual needs of her partner. A father may also find himself neglected by excited friends and family who inquire after the well-being of mother and baby, but express little appreciation for the profound changes affecting him. In general, this is a mild and self-limited mood alteration that does not require treatment but may require the recognition of the father's needs by the preoccupied new mother.

Depression in Midlife

Midlife transitions begin sometime between ages forty and sixty for all of us who live long enough. This is a natural stage of life and represents a maturation process. The naturalness of midlife experiences does not mean that they are not uncomfortable. Midlifers may breeze through this phase of their lives, which bridges the exuberance and impulsiveness of their young adulthood and the settled perspective of the senior years. This period may also, however, prompt a range of feelings from discontent with lifestyle to boredom with activities and people that were once found stimulating. Midlifers experience an urge for change while questioning the meaning of life and the validity of decisions they made as young adults. This is a time of losses—deaths of parents, divorces, the peaking of careers. Yet for many it is a time of relative affluence and health. For some midlifers, this period represents the end of their youth and sexual attractiveness. For others, it is truly the best of times.

Midlife begins earlier for women than for men. It is a well-recognized part of the female life cycle, marked by the physiological stage of menopause, which is anticipated eagerly by some women and dreaded by others. The majority of women go through natural menopause between ages forty-five and fifty-four. As they approach this physical end of reproductive fertility, women in their late thirties and early forties may experience increased concerns about their attractiveness and their changing roles. Women in their forties often feel that they have peaked, that their good years (both sexually and professionally) are behind them.

Although they do not have a similar physical landmark signaling their entrance into midlife, men in their forties and fifties commonly experience the phenomenon popularly known as "midlife crisis." While their fears of peaking out occur ten to twenty years later than women's, men do experience physical changes (such as decreasing muscular strength and sexual performance) in their forties and fifties. These physical changes create self-doubt and sometimes frantic attempts to retain or recapture youth. Midlife is a time when men may suddenly realize that the dreams that have driven them since early adulthood are illusions that promised power and pleasure but returned only a workaholic lifestyle with little personal intimacy.

Robert C. was a fifty-two-year-old married man brought to the emergency room following a self-inflicted gunshot wound to the chest. An upper-level manager with an international manufacturing corporation, he was a self-described workaholic who recently had been passed over for a promotion he had desired. Robert had little family life. His three children were in college and rarely visited. His wife was active in community affairs and had begun working part-time as a realtor once her children had left home. Robert had no hobbies and had never taken time for recreational activities with friends. In the previous year or two, he had begun to experience intense feelings of loneliness and failure in both business and personal arenas. His work performance suffered, and absenteeism became a problem as he began to experience various aches and ailments. His relationship with his wife deteriorated when he demanded that she stay home to care for him. At her suggestion, Robert went to his family physician for treatment of his physical complaints and was referred to a psychiatrist. He angrily refused to accept the referral, drove home, and shot himself in the chest minutes before his wife was due home from work.

While midlife is a time when men and women alike are at risk for depressive episodes, there is no specific form of depression peculiar to midlife, although earlier psychiatric literature described an entity known as involutional melancholia. It was thought to be a severe form of withdrawn depression occurring in midlife. Some physical factors beginning in midlife may predispose individuals to depressive episodes. For example, recent studies have shown that menopausal and postmenopausal women may have increased vulnerability to depression because of hormone changes and that treatment with estrogen replacement therapy may provide some measure of protection against milder forms of depression. Other studies, such as the one done by S. W. Simpson and associates in England, have suggested that serious depression beginning for the first time after age forty may have a different origin. These mid-to-late-life depressions may be related more to "silent" circulatory problems deep within the brain than to a hereditary predisposition to mood disorders, which is the common finding in younger individuals who experience depression.

Depression in Late Life

Depression is not a normal reaction to life circumstances and certainly not a normal part of the aging process. To the contrary, most older people feel satisfied with their lives.

George T. was a sixty-nine-year-old retired chauffeur. During his years of employment, he had led an active and rewarding life as a chauffeur for many wealthy and famous people in Europe and the Caribbean. Although he never married, George fathered several children who grew to adulthood without any relationship with their father. Following his retirement at age sixty-five, George moved back to settle in the rural state of his birth. Accustomed to an extravagant lifestyle, he quickly expended his savings; he had no retirement income. By the age of sixty-nine, he was destitute and living in a boardinghouse where he ate only one meal a day because he could not afford full room and board. His landlady grew concerned and took him to the local mental health center because he seemed confused, had memory problems, and sat alone in his room all day. George was hospitalized for evaluation of dementia. Despite prominent symptoms of memory loss, confusion, and inability to care for himself, George's medical workup, including brain scans, was essentially normal. Treatment was begun with antidepressant medication while social services arranged for him to receive a monthly financial supplement, food stamps, and coverage for medical expenses. Within six weeks, George's memory problems and confusion were substantially resolved.

Late life is another time of losses. People over sixty face losing their spouses, their friends, and even their children. They have to confront the possibility of loss of vigor, loss of health, loss of work, and sometimes loss of financial security. Suicide rates in older people are on the rise, yet symptoms of depression are rarely recognized and treated in this population. As many as nine out of ten older people who have depression do not get treatment for their disorder.

According to the Epidemiologic Catchment Area Study (ECAS) sponsored by the National Institute of Mental Health (U.S.) in the 1980s, depressive symptoms occur in approximately 15 percent of people over sixty-five years of age. At least 3 percent of elderly people suffer serious depression, especially those who reside in nursing homes, where the rate of depression approaches 15 to 25 percent.

The most common symptoms of late-life depression are persistent sadness of greater than two weeks' duration, a feeling of being slowed down, excessive worry over finances or health problems, fretfulness, pacing, physical complaints, sleep problems, tearfulness, feelings of worthlessness or helplessness, difficulty in concentrating, and memory problems. Late-life depressions may involve withdrawal from previous social, hobby-related, and recreational pursuits because the elder has lost interest or does not have the energy. Self-neglect may result in the depressed older person putting less emphasis on personal appearance and hygiene, as well as loss of interest in cooking and eating, with subsequent weight loss.

Tragically, depressed elderly people in nursing homes may appear to be complainers and receive no treatment for their condition. Their depressions are masked because the true nature of the illness is hidden behind a cloak of physical complaints, or else the elderly person avoids describing the symptoms for fear of being labeled "crazy." Elderly patients commonly experience mild memory problems and slowing of mental processes, both conditions resulting from physical causes. When depression develops on top of this mild brain dysfunction, the result often looks like advanced dementia or "old-timer's disease," for which the grieving family assumes there is no treatment. With proper diagnosis and treatment of severe depression, elderly patients often shed the symptoms of this pseudodementia and experience an improvement in both brain function and quality of life.

Two types of depression occur in older people: (1) depression that started earlier in life and relapses in late life, and (2) depression that occurs for the first time in late life. Early onset depression that occurs again in late life usually has genetic factors similar to those in younger people with depression. Depression occurring for the first time in late life commonly is associated with increased rates of chronic medical and neurological disease. People with late-onset depression are particularly subject to brain side effects from medications of all types and to abnormalities associated with medical illnesses.

Late life is frequently complicated by multiple and chronic medical problems that may cause secondary depression or aggravate preexisting depression. Patients, family members, and caregivers may erroneously consider the symptoms a normal response to serious physical illness. There is nothing normal about secondary depression except that serious physical illness is a major life stress, and major life stresses appear to have a role in precipitating depression. Depression in the elderly certainly has the potential to become a lethal physical illness if unrecognized and untreated.

Suicide is more common in the elderly than in any other population group. According to the National Mental Health Association, people over sixty-five account for more than 25 percent of suicides in the United States. Indeed, white men over eighty are six times more likely than the general population to commit suicide. Most depressed people welcome concern and help, but elderly depressed people who are suicidal may avoid revealing the seriousness of their distress because they were reared in a time when psychological issues were not publicly addressed, when people with emotional problems were considered weak or "feeble-minded" and liable to be "put away in a lunatic asylum." The depressed elderly often feel they have outlived their usefulness and have nothing to look forward to, while at the same time they fear being labeled insane and losing whatever control over their lives they may still retain.

Depression Associated with Medical or Surgical Conditions

While chronic medical and surgical problems of any variety may be significant life stressors and therefore associated with depression, certain common physical conditions are especially likely to cause depressive symptoms.

Gina S. was a twenty-eight-year-old woman with a four-month-old baby. She had been a teacher and active community leader until she became pregnant. Having lost her first pregnancy to a miscarriage at three months' gestation, Gina quit work as soon as she became pregnant the second time and planned to devote herself full-time to motherhood. She delivered a healthy baby girl and did well herself until she became irritated with her inability to lose weight following the birth of her child. She fatigued easily and spent most of her time lying in bed tending the baby, watching television, or sleeping. Normally of a happy disposition, Gina became concerned about her increasingly pessimistic frame of mind. Tearful at intervals, she feared she was developing a postpartum depression. One day a physician friend directed Gina's attention to an enlargement at the base of her neck and referred her to an endocrinologist who diagnosed a goiter secondary to hypothyroidism and prescribed thyroid supplementation. Within a few months, Gina lost the excess weight, became active and productive, and was again her normal, content self.

Disease of the thyroid gland, a two-lobed structure in the neck in front of the trachea (windpipe), is a common cause of depression, especially in women. The thyroid gland produces a hormone that influences most of the other parts of the body. When the gland produces too little thyroid hormone, a condition known as hypothyroidism, the body reacts by slowing down its metabolism. The patient feels sluggish and tired all the time, gains weight, gets puffy, and experiences a slowed heart rate, constipation, and changes in skin and hair. The patient may also experience symptoms of mild-to-severe depression including lack of energy, sleep and appetite disturbance, tearfulness, depressed mood, and decreased mental acuity with memory difficulties.

When the gland becomes overactive and produces too much thyroid hormone, many of the body processes speed up, resulting in serious physical ailments affecting the same body systems hypothyroidism does, but with opposite effects. This condition, known as hyperthyroidism, can lead to racing thoughts, mental confusion, and psychosis. Paradoxically, the excessive production of thyroid hormone can also cause major depression.

Cancer is diagnosed in more than 1.3 million Americans each year. Of those individuals, 25 percent will develop significant depressive symptoms. Unrecognized and untreated depression in cancer patients may interfere with their motivation to undertake cancer therapy.

Patients with heart disease are also at increased risk for depression. Approximately 20 percent of people with coronary artery disease suffer depression even before they have a heart attack. In fact, data suggests that people with coronary artery disease who also have serious depression are at greater risk for heart attack. After heart attack, the risk for developing depression rises to between 40 and 65 percent, a factor which in turn leads to worsening of cardiac symptoms and poorer compliance with cardiac treatment. Many authorities report that heart attack survivors with serious depression have a three-to-four-times greater risk of dying within six months than those who do not suffer from depression. It can be argued that the emotional stress of a heart attack may be the factor causing depression and that the more serious the heart attack is, the more likely the survivor is to suffer from depression and a higher mortality in the recovery phase. It is equally likely, however, that stress-related physical changes common in depression, such as increased production of emergency hormones, overwork the damaged heart and produce higher mortality rates. One man who survived a heart attack that was followed by a severe depression commented, "If I have to have one of them again, and I hope I don't, I'd rather have a heart attack."

Each year in the United States almost half a million people suffer strokes. Of those who survive, as many as 25 percent develop significant depression within two months of their stroke. The tendency is, of course, to explain away any mood alteration by citing the physical devastation. The fact is that the severity of physical disability following strokes is not closely associated with the severity of depression that develops afterward. Instead, the tendency to develop depression is more closely associated with strokes on the left side of the brain than with those on its right side, especially when the stroke involves areas closer to the front of the brain. The reasons for this phenomenon are not yet clear.

Other medical conditions frequently associated with depression include abnormalities of the adrenal glands (small glands that sit like caps on top of the kidneys), cancer of the tail of the pancreas (the organ that produces insulin), and a devastating hereditary neurological condition known as Huntington's chorea.

Many medications prescribed for common medical conditions can also cause significant depressions. The most frequent offenders are certain classes of medications used to treat hypertension (high blood pressure) and steroids like cortisone used to treat a myriad of medical conditions, from simple allergic reactions to chronic disorders involving muscle, tendon, and joint discomfort.

Depression in Substance Abusers

Substance abuse disorders (i.e., alcoholism and drug abuse) frequently coexist with depression. Depending on their training, clinicians vary in their opinions as to which is the "chicken" and which is the "egg." Most drugs that are abused, including alcohol, are direct depressants of the nervous system, or else (like cocaine and other stimulants) result in depression of the nervous system once the abuser "crashes" from a sustained chemically induced high. Proponents of traditional alcohol and drug rehabilitation programs adhere to the belief that the chemical abuse of the brain is the primary cause for the depressive symptoms complained of by most chronic substance abusers. They believe abstinence from substances of abuse for an adequate period of "detox" is necessary before an accurate assessment of depression can be performed. They also believe that medical treatment of depressive symptoms in active users is a losing proposition.

Another theory regarding substance abuse and depression is that victims of depression are prone to self-medication with alcohol and drugs, including overmedication with prescription drugs. Adherents of this theory point to data showing that substance abuse disorders occur in 27 percent of people with major depression and 56 percent of those with bipolar disorder. Those clinicians have coined the term "dual diagnosis" to describe people who exhibit significant symptoms of both substance abuse and depression. In cases where both problems are suspected, clinicians recommend that a thorough history be taken from patients as well as from significant others in their lives in order to establish whether mood symptoms predated the onset of substance use. If such is the case, they argue that a dual diagnosis is warranted and that active treatment of depression should be instituted even in the face of continuing active substance abuse so long as precautions are taken to prevent persistent overmedication or purposeful overdose.

Depression Associated with Seasonal Variations

Seasonal mood changes were described over 150 years ago, but were not officially named until 1984 when Norman Rosenthal of the National Institute of Mental Health and his colleagues described the cyclical mood disorder that varied with the seasons of the year and named it seasonal affective disorder, or SAD. Subsequent studies in the United States, Canada, Italy, and Switzerland indicate that as many as 10 to 20 percent of people with recurrent depressive episodes may have a predisposition to seasonal mood swings. Research is hampered by similarities between seasonal affective disorder and other forms of depression. Precise diagnosis of SAD is therefore difficult, a circumstance that complicates the interpretation of research data. As a result, controversy remains as to the existence of a pure form of seasonal mood disorder that is distinct from other forms of depression that may also worsen during holiday seasons when depressed individuals see the joy of others and tend to feel even more alone and despondent.

The current thought is that SAD results from seasonal variations in a person's exposure to sunlight and that, therefore, the frequency of SAD should be highest in populations living closest to the earth's poles and least noticeable in populations living near the equator. There are conflicting results from research on this point.

> Margery L. was a sixty-two-year-old housewife referred by her family physician for evaluation of episodic confusion. The episodes were self-limiting and tended to occur about twice a year after her first severe episode, which occurred when she was in her early twenties. In addition to confusion, Margery experienced slowed thoughts, sleep disturbance, self-doubting, extreme social withdrawal, and depression, but no hallucinations or delusions. Between episodes of severe depression, Margery managed to remain happily married, maintain a household, work full-time, and rear three children to adulthood. Upon questioning, both Margery and her husband independently reported that her worst episodes, including the first, had occurred during "football season," i.e., in the autumn. Milder episodes tended to occur in the spring.

Atypical depressions classified as SAD commonly develop in the autumn (sometimes as early as mid-August), increase in severity during the winter until January, and recede as summer approaches, when the depression clears. An alternate variety of SAD exhibits spring/summer depression instead of autumn/winter depression. A third pattern can result in autumn/winter depressions and summer manic episodes.

The symptoms of SAD, also known as "winter depression" in its milder form, include increased sleepiness, increased appetite (often with craving of carbohydrates) and weight gain, and decreased activity levels with sluggishness. Other symptoms include tearfulness, loss of motivation, and pessimism. In the classic pattern, the symptoms occur regularly during "football season" in the fall and are at their worst in January and February, with relief from depressive symptoms coming in the spring and summer months.

The mood abnormalities seen in SAD are most commonly thought to be a result of seasonal light variations that follow from the changing lengths of the periods of daylight as the earth makes its annual pilgrimage around the sun. Research suggests that, in some people, the pineal gland (fig. 2.1) is highly sensitive to those changes and alters its production of melatonin, a sleep-related hormone, based on the seasonal variations in sunlight. When the days are shorter and darker, the pineal gland increases its production of melatonin, which in turn influences physiological changes in hormonal, immune, and nervous systems, especially those that rely on an internal biological clock, often referred to as a circadian rhythm.

Fifteen years of research at the National Institute of Mental Health implicates melatonin in the development of SAD; however, the exact nature of its role remains unclear, since other neurochemicals, such as serotonin (a neurotransmitter thought

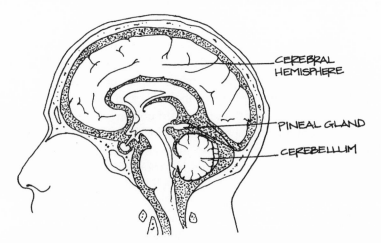

FIG. 2.1. Pineal gland.

to be involved in causing depression), appear to be involved also. Melatonin production is increased during the autumn/winter months. How that translates into the development of a depressive mood remains unclear.

Paul Schwartz, Norman Rosenthal, and Thomas Wehr at the National Institute of Mental Health recently described the existence of a central nervous system "proportional control thermostat" in humans that links the mechanisms governing several body responses to stress, including mood change. The researchers investigated the relationships involving the thermostat, serotonin, melatonin, and winter depression. They noted that serotonin influences the body's responsiveness to light, while melatonin has a major influence on the actions of serotonin throughout the brain. Their complicated neurohormonal study concluded that the thermostat changes reported in SAD and with changes in melatonin production are not found in at least one serotonin-controlled system, the daytime regulation of core temperature (one measure of circadian function controlled by the thermostat). Their study found no abnormality in regulation of core body temperature in patients with SAD. That finding argues against the idea that serotonin is the primary cause of seasonal depressions.

Other causes have been proposed for SAD. Retinal mechanisms have been studied as a possibility, because the retina is the light-sensitive layer of the eye that generates electrical impulses in response to light. Those impulses run along nerve fibers to the visual cortex in the back of the brain. Studies of the retina, however, have produced no consistent association between depression and retinal function in SAD. Preliminary brain-imaging studies using positron emission tomography (PET) have found abnormalities in various areas of the brain in SAD patients, including decreased activity levels in the frontal and left parietal lobes.

Other studies cast some doubt on the retina proposal, suggesting that the skin may be the light-sensitive organ that signals the pineal gland to produce melatonin. If such is the case, a new set of transmitter substances must be involved in the communication between skin and pineal gland.

A. J. Lewy and colleagues proposed in the 1987 issue of *Science* that seasonal variation in natural sunlight has the effect of producing depressive symptoms in winter by causing "phase delays" in the circadian timing systems in individuals predisposed to SAD. They further proposed that seasonal depressions could be counteracted by the antidepressant effect of a "phase advance" caused by exposure to morning light. Their studies suggested that exposure to morning light for two hours per day was more effective at influencing melatonin production as well as at causing clinical improvement in depression than either midday or evening light exposure.

Research is ongoing to identify the critical components of successful light therapy, i.e., wavelength of light, duration of exposure, frequency of exposure, timing of exposure, and even site of exposure. Scott S. Campbell and Patricia J. Murphy of Cornell University Medical College reported in 1998 that light exposure to the back of the knee can alter the circadian rhythm and melatonin levels.

3. The Causes of Depression

"How did I get this way? Was it something I did? Is this some kind of punishment?"

—A minister

We have been striving since earliest times to understand the nature and the causes of the depressive affliction that drastically changes a person's mood and behavior. We continue searching for the answer, yet the exact nature of the illness still eludes us.

Early ideas regarding the nature of depression were products of the predominant philosophies of their times, just as current theories reflect the scientific philosophy of the present time. Ancient writings describing the affliction laid its cause to supernatural intervention, primarily religious in nature. In the Hindu texts, gods personifying good and evil warred with one another and victimized individual humans. In texts from Babylonia and Egypt, gods punished transgressions in the hearts of people and placed on them the depressive curse. The early Hebrew texts allude to the belief that depression in humans reflects the displeasure of Yahweh.

The ancient Greeks, while bound by a polytheistic belief system, were also great innovators of nontheistic philosophies. They wrote detailed descriptions of an illness they called "melancholia." According to their "humoral theory," melancholia was caused by an excess of "black bile." The ancient Greeks also described a melancholic temperament that compares to our current concepts of dysthymic disorder, a milder but often lifelong form of depression.

During the Middle Ages, as in all ages, many people turned to supernatural explanations for mental illness. Depression became God's punishment for sinners or the natural condition of souls under the control of the devil. This was the age of witch hunts, when many unfortunate women and some men were accused of being in league with Satan and severely punished for the sin of mental illness, including depression.

Beginning in the late nineteenth and early twentieth centuries, physicians turned once more to the human body and the human mind in seeking the source of depression. Western scientists such as Emil Kraeplin developed detailed, sophisticated systems for classifying depression based on observations of characteristic symptoms and the course of the illnesses. Sigmund Freud, the renowned Austrian neurologist, developed a concept of mental illness based on "instincts," or natural bodily drives.

The predominant current theories on the origin of depression fall into two major categories, psychosocial and neurobiological. Research supports some aspects of each, but consistently substantiates neither.

Psychosocial Theories

Psychosocial theories, which include psychoanalytic, behavioral, environmental, cognitive, and interpersonal theories, are generally based on observations of human behavior and on philosophical explanations as to how the human mind and human mood and behavior relate. Some, especially behavioral theories, rely to an extent on observations of animal and human behavior, and they are tested by data gathering with standard research models.

Psychoanalytic Theories

Sigmund Freud looked to the mind for the cause of depression and other mental illnesses, eventually developing the school of theory and treatment of mental illness that came to be known as psychoanalysis. He postulated that illnesses of the mind are caused by unconscious conflicts between human instincts (which he called collectively the "id") and the human conscience (which he called the "superego"). His initial theory emphasized the basic role of unsatisfied, primitive sexual drives in developing intolerable levels of anxiety. If acted upon indiscriminately, powerful sexual drives can place individuals in conflict with their environment, causing further distress. Freud proposed that, to avoid such potentially damaging conflicts, individuals often mask their primitive sexual drives by developing characteristic methods to subdue the intolerable levels of anxiety. Freud called these methods "defense mechanisms" and concluded that individuals varied as to which ones they tended to rely on most, accounting for the differing temperaments among humans. He noted that ongoing attempts to balance the demands of the masked sexual drive and the demands of the environment are associated with unrecognized or unconscious conflicts, which themselves tend to produce anxiety. Freud believed that depression results from failure of characteristic defense mechanisms to effectively deal with unconsciously generated anxieties.

Later, Freud and his followers in Europe and the United States elaborated on his theories. Freud and Karl Abraham emphasized the connection between depression and mourning through the individual's conscious and unconscious preoccupation with the lost loved one, especially with the ambivalent feelings they believed are associated with all human relationships.

According to this theory, the anger and aggression associated with an individual's ambivalent feelings for a lost loved one are turned inward against the self, leading to depression. According to psychoanalytic theorists, the impact of early human attachments and loss in early childhood, such as separation from a parent, may predispose the individual to depression in later life when additional losses occur. Theorists also point out that loss of self-esteem is an almost universal phenomenon in significant depressions. They believe the loss of self-esteem arises from an internal conflict between our expectations ("ego ideal") and the realities of our lives.

In simpler terms, the psychoanalytic theory explains depression as a result of the individual's inability to effectively deal with significant loss and with largely unexpressed and frequently unrecognized anger. Modern therapists who subscribe to this theory believe that the loss and unexpressed rage may be related to significant events other than loss of relationships, such as, for example, being passed over for a desired promotion, being the victim of an assault, being involved in a serious accident, losing financial security, or failing academically.

Behavioral Theories

Behaviorists believe that humans, like other animals, react to their environment and learn from the success or failure of behaviors in dealing with it. Behaviorists theorize that humans come into the world as a blank slate, or tabula rasa, on which their experiences write the scripts for their lives. Behavioral theorists focus on the individual's tendency to overrespond to loss of social supports. When the social environment no longer supports individuals and no longer reinforces their behavior, feelings of isolation, discomfort, and fear result. Behaviorists believe that the lack of social support is one of the strongest factors in the production of depression. They point to a vicious cycle that can intensify and prolong the depression. Depressed people tend to elicit negative responses from important people in their lives, such as their spouses, children, and friends. Eventually tiring of dealing with the depressed person's behaviors, people who have tried to be supportive become less sympathetic and more impatient.

Some behaviorists also believe that people who are prone to depression have impaired social skills, which makes it difficult for them to obtain the level of support and reinforcement they require from their social environment. Over time, according to this theory, people prone to depression tend to experience more negative responses from other people and have less ability to cope with the negativity than do individuals who are not prone to depression.

Environmental Theories

No matter what the philosophy of the times and the explanations given for the origin of depression, people throughout the ages have instinctively connected catastrophic life events to the onset of depression, just as the Hebrews described King Saul's wish for death at the time of his greatest military defeat and the loss of his son in battle. Historians and poets have long connected bouts of melancholia or depression to unrequited love or disastrous love affairs.

Modern studies seem to indicate that the likelihood of depression increases five to six times in the six months following a stressful life event, yet most people who experience a severe life stress do not develop depression. Although the relationship between life stress and the onset of depression is not entirely coincidental, the connection is not a strong one. The lack of a consistent link between stressful events and the onset of depression leads most theorists to believe factors other than stress account for the development of depression.

Some studies suggest that early stressful life events (such as parental loss, emotional or physical deprivation, or physical, sexual, or emotional abuse) may sensitize humans so that they are more likely to develop depression in later life in response to significant stresses. One model that attempts to explain this phenomenon is the "kindling-sensitization" hypothesis, which proposes that, just as repeated exposure to poison ivy may eventually result in an allergy to the noxious plant, repeated stresses tend to sensitize the areas of the brain specializing in emotional responses (the limbic system) so that the cumulative effects of stresses over time produce the mood and behavioral alterations we know as depression.

Cognitive Theories

Cognitive theories emphasize the importance of the ways in which people think about life and themselves. According to cognitive theorists, mood is related to the individual's belief system. In other words, we are what we believe. When our beliefs are pessimistic in nature and we focus on what is wrong or negative in ourselves and our environment rather than on what is good, the natural outcome is a depressive posture. Aaron Beck in 1974 described a cognitive triad for depression: (1) negative view of self, (2) negative interpretation of experiences, and (3) negative expectations of the future. In Beck's model, depression is caused by individuals' negative views of themselves, their world, and their future. According to this theory, depression is not the primary illness but a secondary manifestation of a pessimistic belief system. Cognitive theorists subscribe to the notion that people prone to depression are the same people who tend to see the glass of water as half empty rather than half full.

Learned helplessness and learned hopelessness are features of cognitive theories. People with learned helplessness tend to believe that stressful events are permanent rather than temporary and drastically affect their whole life experience rather than only a component of their lives. They are then naturally overwhelmed by the enormity of life stresses from childhood throughout their adult lives and hopeless about their ability to deal with life on their own.

Cognitive theorists believe that once people assume the typical pessimistic stance presaging depression, then they tend to view all life circumstances in the same manner. As a result, individuals rehearse their beliefs and behaviors and see each circumstance that blends easily with their belief system as yet another proof of the truth of those beliefs. At the same time, they conveniently discard any circumstance that does not fit. In this manner, depressed people learn and maintain their depressive stance through rehearsal and reinforcement. The natural outcome of such a belief system is low self-esteem, self-doubt, a tendency to ruminate about past unhappy experiences, decreased pleasure capacity, and pessimism about the future—all common symptoms of depression.

Interpersonal Theories

One school of thought regarding the cause of depression focuses on the interactions between mood and personal relationships with our environment and with others. Adolf Meyer, Harry Stack Sullivan, Erich Fromm, and Frieda Fromm-Reichmann emphasized the importance of current experiences, relationships, social roles, environmental changes, and life stresses in the cause of emotional disorders. They were inclined to place more emphasis on the "here and now" as a generator of present mood than on the impact of early life experiences.

The connection between depression and interpersonal relationship problems is circular. In other words, we are again confronted with the "chicken or egg" phenomenon of causality. Interpersonal theorists point to deficits in relationship and communication skills as possible precursors of depression. At the same time, depressed people are particularly vulnerable to relationship conflicts and losses as a secondary effect of their mood disorder, which can cause lack of energy, irritability, decreased sex drive, increased physical complaints, sleep and appetite disturbances, withdrawal from people and activities, and loss of pleasure capacity.

Neurobiological Theories

Neurobiological theories include genetic, neurotransmitter, neurohormonal, and biological rhythm theories. Other, less prominent, biological theories, such as the viral theory, have been proposed. Those theories have generally arisen out of research on animals and humans using the scientific method of observation, generation, and evaluation of data.

Genetic Theories

Behavioral genetics is the study of the role of genes in behavior. Behavioral geneticists search for hereditary patterns in depression. The eventual goal is to identify genes that predispose individuals to mood disorders. Because of the differences in the various forms of depression, it seems unlikely that any single gene or gene combination will be found to be responsible for all forms of depression.

Studies of twins have been effective for researching the role of genetic factors in the cause of diseases, including depression. If illnesses like depression are hereditary, then they should be coincident more often in twins who share identical genetic material (identical twins) than in twins who share the same amount of genetic material as ordinary siblings (fraternal, or nonidentical, twins). Studies that use twins who have been separated from birth or early age and reared in different environments can test the role of environmental factors in various conditions.

Many such studies have confirmed a genetic predisposition in most forms of depression. For example, if one parent has a major depressive disorder, the risk to the offspring has been found to be 25 to 30 percent. If both parents have a mood disorder and one is bipolar, the risk of a mood disorder in the offspring may be as high as 50 to 75 percent. The risk is even greater when there is a strong history of multiple generations of mood-disordered family members. Nearly two-thirds of bipolar patients have a positive family history of mood disorders. The exact nature and significance of this predisposition is not yet clear.

Recent gene-mapping studies using recombinant DNA suggest the presence of a single mutation causing bipolar disorder in some families. The known gene mutations differ in different families and are not present in all bipolars.

Even if a specific gene can be identified as producing a predisposition to a mood disorder, how would it cause the symptoms of the disorder? One possibility is that the gene will encode for the synthesis of an enzyme (such as tyrosine hydroxylase) vital to the production of neurotransmitters involved in mood disorders.

Neurotransmitter Theories

Most biological research on depression focuses on the role of chemicals in the brain that transmit information and instructions from one brain cell to another. Those chemicals are called neurotransmitters. Many neurotransmitters have been identified and many more await discovery. These theories generally hold that depression is caused by abnormalities in or inadequate levels of one or more neurotransmitters.

Such an explanation is deceptively simple, considering the complexity of the nervous system, yet the components of the brain can be reduced to a relatively simple model consisting of a cell that is specialized to receive, process, and transmit information. The nerve receives information from many other nerves, integrates it, and transmits it to other cells. Some nerve cells or neurons send signals to activate other cells, while some signal cells to turn off activities. Some neurons add impulses from adjacent nerve cells until they reach a threshold sufficient to fire signals of their own. Others require only a single impulse to fire and thus operate on a simple "off or on" principle. The signal that moves along the cell body is electrical in nature and is started by the movement of charged elements (ions) such as sodium, potassium, and calcium into and out of the cell body. The transmission of information from one neuron to those adjacent features a process known as neurotransmission, involving neurotransmitter chemicals such as serotonin in the spaces (synaptic clefts) between nerve cells. It is that process of neurotransmission that is modified by antidepressant medications.

Neurotransmitter research has focused largely on the effects of the chemicals on the activity of regions of the brain and the resulting displays of mood and behavior. Medical techniques cannot yet cope with the complexity of the human nervous system, with its perplexing interplay of various neurotransmitters and electrical and biochemical reactions within the millions of cells that form the highly specialized, interdependent tissues of the central nervous system.

"I have a chemical imbalance" is a common explanation for depression. That is both a truth and an enormous oversimplification.

Neurohormonal Theories

Some hormones have significant effects on brain function, and when they are present in abnormally low or high levels they may have deleterious effects. A common example involves the depressed mood and slowing of thought processes often experienced by people whose thyroid glands do not produce sufficient thyroid hormone. The result can be a severe depression that has all the negative effects of other severe depressions, including increased risk for suicide. On the other hand, thyroid abnormalities are not present in all individuals with severe depressive episodes. Other hormone systems entwined with brain function and mood include the adrenal gland hormones, growth hormone, and sex hormones.

Biological Rhythm Theories

Abnormalities in biological rhythms are among the most consistent experiences in depression. Changes in sleep patterns, for example, are frequently the first sign of a major mood disorder. People with depression commonly either experience insomnia or else sleep excessively (hypersomnia). Research on sleeping and awake individuals is done by connecting them to various machines that monitor brain wave activity, eye movement, breathing, and heartbeat. Such research demonstrates that human sleep is not a homogeneous period of shut-eye, when both the body and the brain are shut down. In fact, while we sleep our brains go through predictable patterns of activity that can be tracked with an electroencephalogram (EEG), an instrument that measures brain wave activity. Polysomnography, the study of sleep patterns and their abnormalities, utilizes simultaneous monitoring of brain wave activity (via an EEG), breathing, and body movements.

A normal sleep cycle involves repeating patterns of four stages of gradually slowing brain activity associated with essentially no rapid eye movement (non-REM sleep) and one stage of greater brain activity associated with rapid eye movements visible to an observer (REM sleep). Dreaming is thought to occur primarily during REM sleep. The phases of non-REM sleep are called stages 1, 2, 3, and 4 and are followed by the stage of REM sleep. Adults spend about 50 percent of their sleep time in stage 2 sleep, about 20 percent in REM sleep, and the remaining 30 percent in the other stages of non-REM sleep. Infants, by contrast, spend about half their sleep time in REM sleep. The amount of time spent by adults in each stage varies as sleep progresses; by early morning, individuals spend proportionally more time in REM and stages 1 and 2 sleep. The first REM sleep of the night usually occurs about 70 to 90 minutes after going to sleep. A complete sleep cycle, including four non-REM stages and one REM stage, lasts an average of 90 to 110 minutes. Most adults spend an average of two hours per night in REM sleep and presumably dreaming, although they often cannot recall their dreams.

The pattern of sleep cycling is altered in depressed patients. Polysomnography demonstrates that the progression of sleep stages in them is disrupted. One of the most common changes found in depressed individuals is the tendency to enter REM sleep (and presumably begin dreaming) more quickly after they fall asleep than do nondepressed people. They also exhibit increased frequency of eye movements during REM sleep. Non-REM sleep abnormalities include difficulty initiating sleep (prolonged latency in onset of stage 1 sleep), more frequent arousals that lead to a reduction in total sleep time as well as in time spent in deep sleep (stages 3 and 4), and earlier awakenings.

Other biological rhythm changes that may be associated with depression include abnormalities in the daily patterns of adrenal hormone secretions and body temperature. Seasonal variations in mood patterns, or seasonal affective disorder (SAD), occur in some depression-prone people, as described in chapter 2.

Social Rhythm Theories

Social rhythm theories, which combine aspects of psychosocial theory and biological principles, hold that biological rhythms of life are intimately entwined with our physical and emotional well-being. They suggest that social relationships, regular working habits, or the routine of life tend to support the stability of biological rhythms and the total biological entity, a condition known as homeostasis. Disruption of social relationships, work, or life routines therefore tends to destabilize biological rhythms such as sleep and temperature cycles and appetite patterns. The resulting disruptions of neurobiological processes can potentially lead to the thought, emotional, and behavior changes associated with depression.

Other Biological Theories

Borna disease virus (BDV) was named for the town in Saxony, Germany, where in 1766 horses were diagnosed with a mysterious ailment now sometimes referred to as "sad horse" disease (equine encephalitis). The disease is common in animals in Europe but not in the United States. Human infections with the virus also are more common in Europe. The Borna disease virus causing the illness is a single-strand RNA virus that replicates in nerve cells. It infects many different species of animals, both wild and domesticated, and in some causes neurological and behavioral changes. Behavioral changes include both aggressive and passive stages. Those biphasic manifestations in animals led to hypotheses that BDV could be related to mood disorders in humans, and the search for BDV in humans commenced.

Human infection with BDV was first described in the mid-1990s when German researchers recovered antibodies for the virus in samples taken from four patients with depressive symptoms (three in Germany and one in the United States). Viral proteins and antibodies tended to appear during or near episodes of depression, suggesting that the virus can promote depression when it is activated from a dormant state.

The incubation period for Borna disease (BD) in horses and sheep is four weeks. In animals, the mode of spread appears to be by direct contact and exposure to the virus via saliva and nasal secretions. Transmission of the disease by insect vectors has been postulated, because BD tends to occur in spring and early summer and is more common in some years than in others. BDV, however, has never been isolated from insects in Europe. In the Near East, ticks have been found to transmit a virus similar to BD. A definite reservoir for BDV has not been found, but rodents represent the most likely one. In addition, animals with subclinical infections can be potential sources of infection for other animals and for humans. Direct transmission of the BD virus from horse to human has been documented in at least one case in Europe in which a man contracted an illness caused by BDV after going to work on a horse farm. Scientists doubt that BDV can be acquired by humans from eating meat or other products of infected animals. Treatment for the viral illness is not yet available.

Although the hypothesis of a viral etiology for depression is interesting and the subject of ongoing research, it is by no means confirmed. Many animals with antibodies to BDV show no neurological or behavioral abnormality. Emerging reports provide inconsistent findings with regard to the presence of BDV antibodies in humans with depression and those with no neurological or psychiatric problems. Scientists suspect that the infection causes no problem in most people, but may bring on depressive episodes in those predisposed by genetic or other factors.

While the reports are intriguing, the possibility of a viral cause for some depression has not received widespread acceptance in the scientific community. Further research is needed to clarify the relationship between viral infections and depression.

As the twentieth century draws to a close, research continues with increasing fervor into the cause of major depressive illness. None of the current theories explains all aspects of depression, yet each has some validity. What is the closest we can come to a workable theory regarding the cause of depression? Perhaps it is the commonly held and previously described notion of the fertile ground theory, which holds that hereditary or biological vulnerability and significant life stresses combine to produce a depressive episode. Ultimately, research (see chapter 7) indicates that all depressions appear to involve alterations in brain chemistry; thus, most sufferers should respond to antidepressant medications.

4. What Happens in the Brain

"I feel like my brain has turned to mush. Like it's broken. Like it's dying."

—A medical student

Depression is not a philosophical response to the circumstances of life. Physical changes occur in the brains and bodies of individuals who suffer from serious depression.

The brain is active from before birth until death, but it does not signal its activity with flashing lights in neon hues reminiscent of television ads. The brain does not pulsate, nor does it conveniently broadcast its thoughts through electronic amplification systems in the manner familiar to devotees of horror movies. To the contrary, the brain sits invisible in a cavern of bone known as the skull. If a portion of the skull is cut away to allow the curious to peer inside, the living brain can be seen sitting inert in its tight semitransparent coat, bathed in fluid and fed by blood vessels. It's not a particularly impressive sight, and yet the living brain is the seat of humanness, the organ that makes us who we are. Until recently, the living human brain was studied far less than were the organs that pump, pulsate, filter, or secrete. The activity of the brain is much more subtle than that of the other organs and is less understood, lying enshrouded in mystery, myth, and misunderstanding.

The Normal Brain and Its Functions

The brain is not a homogeneous mass of tissue, a "thinking muscle." Instead it is composed of interconnected, interdependent parts with different structures and different functions. Although all normal human brains share roughly the same construction and shape (fig. 4.1), no two human brains are exactly alike.

The interior portions are thought to be the oldest parts of the brain as far as human evolution is concerned and as a group are sometimes referred to as the paleobrain (fig. 4.2). The inner structures appear much the same in all mammals. The paleobrain includes the medulla and the pons, which together contain the central control systems for most of the functions necessary for life, including the centers for regulating consciousness, breathing, blood pressure, and body temperature.

At the back of the brain sitting on top and behind the pons is the cerebellum (fig. 4.3). The cerebellum comprises two hemispheres, or halves, joined at the center. The cerebellum is primarily involved with coordinating body movements, but research has hinted at additional, more subtle coordinating functions.

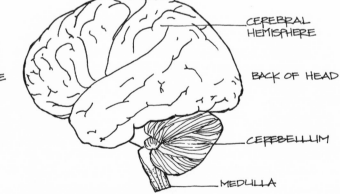

FIG. 4.1. Human brain (side view).

Also connected to the paleobrain but sitting above it are deeper structures of the brain, known, for obvious reasons, as the midbrain. The midbrain contains the hypothalamus, an important center for control of essential bodily functions such as eating, drinking, and reproduction, as well as regulation of the endocrine glands. The hypothalamus functions as a way station for many brain activities and is connected to almost all of the other parts of the brain.

Located on the underside of the brain and connected to the hypothalamus is a small structure called the pituitary gland, which acts as a communications substation between the hypothalamus and many other parts of the body.

Surrounding the midbrain on top and on all sides is the most recently developed part, the cerebrum, which makes up the organ's exterior and gives the human brain its familiar appearance. The cerebrum is most highly developed in the human species and is the seat of the highest mental functions. It is divided laterally into two large, relatively symmetrical halves, or hemispheres, separated front to back by a deep fissure. The hemispheres are joined underneath by a communicating structure called the corpus callosum (fig. 4.4). The hemispheres and convoluted surface of the cerebrum bear some physical resemblance to a shelled walnut half.

As a general rule, the left cerebral hemisphere contains the dominant areas for specialized functions such as language, calculation, logic, planning, and sequencing. It also controls movement on the right side of the body. The right hemisphere is more specialized for musical abilities, spatial skills, and understanding of nonverbal symbols. In addition, it controls the left side of the body.

Each cerebral hemisphere is subdivided into four major portions known as lobes (fig. 4.5), which have specialized functions. From front to back, the lobes of each hemisphere are the frontal lobe (behind the forehead and the eyes), the parietal lobe (at the top and upper portions of the side of the head), the occipital lobe (at the back of the head), and the temporal lobe

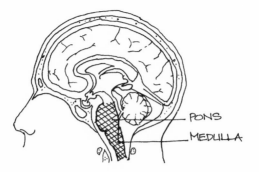

FIG. 4.2. Paleobrain.

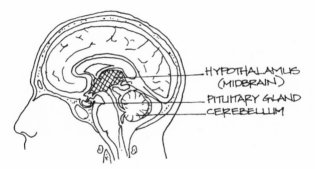

FIG. 4.3. Deep structures of the brain.

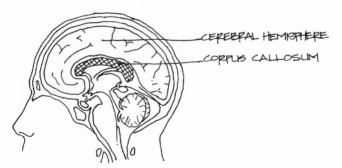

FIG. 4.4. Cerebrum and corpus callosum.

(in the area stretching from the temple back toward the rear of the brain).

The frontal lobes are the largest, making up almost one third of the brain's surface. In many respects, it is the enhanced development of the frontal lobes that distinguishes human brains from those of other animals. This region of the brain is concerned with higher intellectual functioning, including so-called "executive functions," i.e., skills related to monitoring, planning, initiating, and inhibiting complex behaviors. The frontal lobes also contain the major areas of the brain that deal with voluntary body movements, speech, and some aspects of mood. The prefrontal area of the brain has extensive connections to other areas of the brain responsible for controlling the neurotransmitters (dopamine, norepinephrine, and serotonin) and is thought to be important in regulating mood by acting as a set of brakes for emotional responses.

The parietal lobes are primarily concerned with interpreting and integrating information obtained through the five senses—smell, taste, vision, hearing, and touch—as well as imparting awareness of the body's location in its immediate space. The

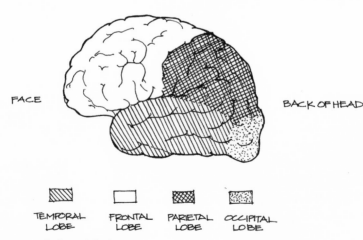

FACE   BACK OF HEAD

| TEMPORAL LOBE | FRONTAL LOBE | PARIETAL LOBE | OCCIPITAL LOBE |

FIG. 4.5. Lobes of the brain.

occipital lobes, the smallest of the four divisions, are located at the back of the brain and are primarily concerned with vision. The temporal lobes are involved with memory formation, emotional reactivity, and processing of sounds and smells.

The Limbic System

The limbic system, in popular science literature, is the "seat of human emotion." The reality, of course, is more complex. The limbic system is an interconnected circuit of brain structures involved in emotional responses. Included in the circuit are the hypothalamus and its prominent connections to the frontal and temporal lobes of the brain. Complex emotions such as pleasure, friendliness, love, and affection as well as more "primitive" emotions such as aversion, fear, anger, rage, and aggression, result from activation of the limbic system.

Messenger Systems of the Brain

The structures of the brain are interconnected through a complex network of nerve bundles. Chemicals called neurotransmitters transmit data from one neuron to the next when they are released into the small cleft (synapse) between the transmitter nerve cell and the receiver nerve cell. The neurotransmitter then attaches to receptors located on the receiver nerve cell, culminating message transmission.

The most studied neurotransmitters are dopamine (DA), norepinephrine (NE), serotonin (5HT), acetyl choline (ACh), and GABA (fig. 4.6). These chemical messengers, stimulating cells in tandem, send instructions from one part of the brain to another and activate, modulate, or discontinue activities of targeted clusters of brain cells.

Biological Abnormalities in Depression

Knowledge of the brain and its functions expanded in the latter quarter of the twentieth century. Researchers discovered

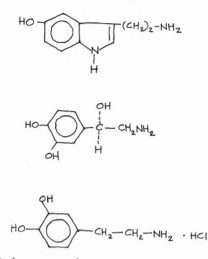

FIG. 4.6. Chemical structure of neurotransmitters: (a) serotonin, (b) norepinephrine, (c) dopamine.

changes in the mind/body connections and function of people with serious depression. Although there are still numerous missing puzzle pieces, some recently discovered alterations in anatomy, in chemistry, and in function seem significant.

Early studies looking for biological associations with depression were forced to deal mainly with anatomical changes because of the complexity of the brain and the relative lack of information about brain anatomy and chemistry. Much of the research was conducted on animals and humans with head injuries and on humans with a specific form of epilepsy thought to originate from damage to the temporal lobes. Those conditions were selected for study because head injuries and temporal lobe epilepsy are often associated with emotional disturbances.

Advances in technology, including assay methods capable of identifying specific receptor sites and imaging techniques such as positron emission tomography (PET), single photon emission computed tomography (SPECT), and, most recently, functional magnetic resonance imaging (ƒMRI, which is potentially more available and cost effective), have allowed researchers to identify activity levels in various brain regions associated with different mental and physical activities. The brain imaging techniques most commonly used by clinicians today remain computerized tomography (CT) and magnetic resonance imaging (MRI) because of availability and cost.

Computerized tomography (CT) scans visualize the brain by measuring differences in the density of different tissue components (cerebrospinal fluid, blood, bone, gray matter, and white matter). Data is obtained by passing X-ray photons through the brain onto a detector. The data is then transmitted to a computer that generates a three-dimensional view of the brain at various levels. A CT scan is used when brain abnormalities such as mass lesions (tumors, abscesses, and hemorrhages), calcifications, atrophy, areas of infarction, or boney abnormalities in the skull are suspected. Details of brain tissue and abnormalities in the area of the brain stem and the cerebellum are not well visualized by CT scanning techniques.

Magnetic resonance imaging (MRI) relies on the use of a magnet and radio waves similar to AM/FM radio waves. It produces detailed images of brain anatomy at different levels so that the scan resembles a fine hand-drawn pen-and-ink illustration. The data is processed by a computer to produce three-dimensional images of the brain at various levels. MRI produces images that are superior to CT scans in differentiating white matter from gray matter and in defining individual brain structures. Because CT scans are more readily available in most medical facilities, and because they are cheaper than MRI scans, CTs remain the brain imaging technique of choice unless the clinician suspects a small lesion in an area that is difficult to visualize and in cases in which a demyelinating (destruction of the protective sheath surrounding nerves) condition such as multiple sclerosis is suspected.

A recent elaboration of MRI scanning is the functional MRI (*f*MRI). That scan allows visualization of the anatomy of the brain as well as its activity in response to predetermined stimuli, such as instructions to move a finger or imagine a sad scene. The *f*MRI uses one of four techniques, but most commonly relies on differences in the magnetic properties of oxygenated red blood cells (as compared to nonoxygenated red blood cells) in order to measure regional differences in oxygen use by brain tissue. Brain tissue engaged in tasks requires more oxygen than brain tissue "on standby." The *f*MRI thus indicates which parts of the brain are using increased amounts of oxygen and, by inference, are more active. Unlike positron-emission tomography and single photon emission computed tomography, the *f*MRI is not invasive and does not involve the injection of radioactive materials.

Positron-emission tomography (PET) and single photon emission computed tomography (SPECT) both provide multicolored images roughly correlating colors with the level of activity in specific areas of the brain, but do not yield precise anatomic images of the brain. Both scanning techniques, which are invasive, require injection of a mildly radioactive organic compound (such as glucose or oxygen) into the bloodstream and track the compound to the brain tissues that absorb the compound from the blood. Active brain cells use more glucose than inactive ones, so active regions of the brain consume larger amounts of radioactive glucose and show up on the PET and SPECT scans as intensely colored areas.

In 1994, Dr. Robert G. Robinson from the University of Iowa reported that patients with damage in specific areas of the left half of the brain, especially in the left frontal lobe, are at significantly increased risk for depression compared with patients in whom damage occurs in other parts of the brain. This finding has been confirmed by other groups using brain imaging techniques such as CT and MRI scans. Dr. Robinson concluded that depression may be caused by episodic misfiring of areas of the left frontal lobe and the left temporal lobe as a result of "genetic, environmental, social, or physiological factors." That conclusion coincides with clinical observations that stroke patients are at greater risk for depression if the stroke is on the left side of the brain, especially in the left frontal lobe.

The majority of recent functional imaging studies have demonstrated a reduction in activity most pronounced in the left prefrontal cortical and limbic areas in individuals with recurrent or chronic depressive disorders. The reduction in activity level is evidenced by decreased blood flow with decreased oxygen or glucose utilization in those neuroanatomical areas.

Dr. Wayne Drevets, a researcher at the University of Pittsburgh Medical Center, recently reported that depressed patients lose substantial brain tissue. Using PET, Dr. Drevets and his colleagues at Washington University and the University of Iowa found that activity in the prefrontal cortex is decreased in individuals with depression. They have also demonstrated a reduction in frontal lobe gray matter, an average of 39 percent reduction in people with bipolar and 48 percent in people with unipolar depression.

What is not yet clear is whether the reduction in gray matter volume in the prefrontal areas is a developmental problem or the result of recurrent illness. Also unknown is whether successful treatment of depression with antidepressants reverses the brain tissue loss.

The first modern biological models for chemical abnormalities in depression gained prominence in the middle of the twentieth century. They proposed that low brain levels of a specific chemical or neurotransmitter cause depression. Research focused on determining which of the commonly recognized neurotransmitters—norepinephrine (NE), dopamine (DA), and serotonin (5-hydroxytryptamine, or 5-HT)—was important in the genesis of depression. Because of the observation that people treated for hypertension with an NE-depleting drug called reserpine tend to develop depression, the first chemical imbalance hypothesis involved inadequate levels of NE in the central nervous system (brain and spinal cord) as the cause of depression.

Eventually researchers began to suspect that depression might involve imbalances among neurotransmitter systems rather than an abnormality of one. The two neurotransmitters currently thought to be most prominent in depression are norepinephrine and serotonin. The levels of those chemicals and their breakdown products usually are measured in the cerebrospinal fluid (CSF) bathing the brain and spinal cord. For example, low levels of norepinephrine and its breakdown products are often found in the CSF of depressed patients, and concentrations of serotonin in the CSF tend to be lower in patients who attempt suicide. Low levels of CSF serotonin also have been found in association with impulsive, violent behavior even when the behavior is not attributable to depression.

Recent studies suggest a complex system in which neurotransmitters signal nerve cells to release other neurotransmitters while the nerve cells that produce them are being simultaneously stimulated by other brain chemicals to increase or diminish the output of the original neurotransmitter. Those findings led to new theories involving "second-messenger" systems in which secondary chemicals affect the synthesis and transport of primary neurotransmitters so that cells are activated in series.

Research into primary neurotransmitter systems led to a revolution in the treatment of depression beginning in the mid-1950s with the emergence of the first effective antidepressant medications. It continues into the present with the development of newer, safer, and equally effective antidepressants (see chapter 7).

Research has identified more than thirty peptides (small proteins) active in the central nervous system (CNS). They are all thought to be neurotransmitters, because they are localized within discrete neurons of the CNS. Many of them are also found in other parts of the body outside the central nervous system. The peptide neurotransmitters include substance P, enkephalins, and ß-endorphin.

Substance P is a neuropeptide that was discovered in 1931. It was initially thought to play a primary role in the transmission of chronic pain signals to the brain. Recently, substance P has become the subject of research on depression. Some investigators believe that the peptide neurotransmitter, which is present in high concentrations in the temporal lobes—an integral part of the limbic system—may play a significant role in the development of depression. In support of this contention is research showing that chronic administration of lithium, a mood stabilizer, increases the levels of substance P in the brains of rats. Other researchers in the area of depression, however, take issue with the conclusions regarding depression and substance P, believing that research findings linking the peptide and depression may be the result of serotonin or norepinephrine activity that was not accounted for in the research model. Pharmaceutical companies have thrown their support behind the research on substance P in hopes of developing an entirely new line of antidepressant medications that are substance P blockers. The success of their efforts has been limited thus far.

Under stress, humans produce a long polypeptide molecule that is broken down by enzymes into a molecule of norepinephrine, one of insulin, and several endorphins and enkephalins—all thought to have neurotransmitter activity in the CNS. The latter two types of neuropeptides have opiate-like qualities. Both bind to the same CNS receptors as opium and its derivatives (including heroin, methadone, morphine, and codeine).

Enkephalins are small proteins (pentapeptides) found in the brain, the spinal cord, and the gastrointestinal tract. Enkephalin levels in the brain have been shown to be increased both by chronic lithium administration and by increasing doses of lithium, while the number of opiate receptors in the brain are apparently decreased by lithium administration. Brain enkephalin levels are also increased following treatment with antidepressant medications and with electroconvulsive therapy. Research indicates that enkephalins may play a role in the development of depression but do not appear to be a significant factor.

Endorphins are also small proteins that bind to opiate receptors in various areas of the brain to produce a potent analgesic effect. Several psychiatric disorders, including unipolar depression (and, to a lesser extent, bipolar depression), are associated with alterations in multiple neurohormonal levels, including ß-endorphin levels. ß-endorphin is secreted from the anterior portion of the pituitary gland in response to release of corticotropin releasing factor (CRF) from the hypothalamus. Stress activates the system, increasing the CNS levels of both CRF and ß-endorphin. The same occurs in drug-free depressed and bipolar depressed patients. ß-endorphin appears to be involved in the central nervous system CRF-circuit that coordinates the endocrine, autonomic, behavioral, emotional, and immune responses to stress in mammals and perhaps to depression in humans.

Depression and the Brain

Depression changes many brain functions. It slows thoughts, making concentration and memory retrieval difficult, and ultimately can lead to psychosis and to a state that looks much like confusion. The illness alters the way depressed people feel about themselves, their circle of friends and family, and their world. It substitutes pessimism, hopelessness, helplessness, and despair for normal attitudes. Depression even alters brain functions that regulate the basic needs of the body, such as those for sleep, food, and sex.

Recent studies indicate that depression is also associated with alterations in the structure of parts of the brain. Whether the structural changes precede the mood changes or vice versa is the subject of scientific debate. Changes in structure have been described in both the hypothalamus and the pituitary of some depressed people. For example, the pituitary gland has been shown by MRI scans to be enlarged in depressed patients. Research has not yet revealed whether the increased size of the pituitary gland is a consistent finding in depression, whether it is permanent, and whether the structural abnormality is the cause or the effect of the illness.

Depression and the Thyroid Gland

Depression changes not only how the brain functions but also how much of the rest of the body functions. Many glands in the body produce hormones that have significant effects on brain function and can cause serious problems when present in abnormal amounts.

As discussed in chapter 2, the most common example of hormone-related depression is the one found in people whose thyroid glands do not produce sufficient thyroid hormone, the condition commonly known as hypothyroidism. Depression caused by hypothyroidism usually responds to daily intake of thyroid hormone supplement. Sometimes thyroid hormone supplementation is even helpful for stabilizing mood disorders occurring in patients with normal levels of circulating thyroid hormone. Many psychiatrists believe that women are more likely than men to benefit from this treatment strategy, because hypothyroidism is more common in women than in men but may go unrecognized when it is mild. A mild deficiency of thyroid hormone is sufficient to aggravate depression.

Depression caused by hypothyroidism may result from an abnormal interaction between thyroid hormone production and production of neurohormones by the hypothalamus and the pituitary gland. There are even indications that different forms of depression may be associated with different patterns of thyroid-pituitary-hypothalamic involvement.

Depression and the Adrenal Glands

The adrenal glands, too, are affected by depression. These glands, which sit like twin caps atop the kidneys, produce several hormones, including hormones affecting stabilization of body fluids and salts, metabolism of glucose, and mobilization of the body's emergency responses. Adrenal gland disorders, such as Cushing's disease, which produce excess amounts of some adrenal hormones, often result in depression. Severe depression, in turn, has been found to increase the production of adrenal hormones normally associated with stressful states in the absence of adrenal gland pathology. Autopsies of suicide victims have tended to find enlargement of the adrenal glands in those who were depressed as evidenced by review of their medical histories.

The adrenal glands are regulated by a feedback loop involving the pituitary gland and the hypothalamus, the HPA axis. Corticotropin releasing factor (CRF) produced by the hypothalamus triggers production of ACTH (adrenocorticotropic hormone) by the anterior portion of the pituitary gland, which in turn causes the adrenal gland to produce glucocorticoids, steriods that are involved with many bodily activities, including glucose metabolism, stress reactions, and immune function. High levels of glucocorticoids in the bloodstream result in decreased production of CRF. CRF has been found to be elevated in the spinal fluid of depressed patients. Blood levels of glucocorticoids are also often elevated in depressives. Studies of the brains of depressed people have shown decreased sensitivity of the frontal lobes to chemicals produced in the hypothalamic-pituitary-adrenal system. In addition, the system is affected by concentrations of the common neurotransmitters serotonin, norepinephrine, acetyl choline, and GABA, chemicals thought to be intimately involved with mood states like depression. Research suggests that different forms of depression affect this neurohormonal system differently.

Depression and Growth Hormone

A third major hormone involved with depression is growth hormone. Growth hormone is produced in the pituitary gland and, as the name implies, assists in the regulation of growth. It is also involved in other functions such as the regulation of glucose metabolism and maintenance of sleep-wake cycles. Production of growth hormone is regulated to some degree by the hypothalamus and the classic neurotransmitters norepinephrine, serotonin, and dopamine.

In nondepressed people, growth hormone is released in pulses that are highest in the early hours of night. In depressed individuals, however, the cycle is altered, with decreased production of growth hormone at night and exaggerated production during the day. Research into the role of growth hormone in depression is inconsistent because of the many factors that influence the system, including sex, phase of menstrual cycle, age, and body weight.

Depression and the Sex Glands

The significance of depression in altering the function of the hormonal axis involving the hypothalamus, the pituitary gland, and the gonads (sex glands) is uncertain. For decades, woman have been known to be at higher risk for depression than men from the time of puberty at least through menopause. Many women also experience temporary mood variations associated with the premenstrual phase of their monthly cycles. These observations suggest that at least one of the female hormones produced by the ovaries may be a factor in depression. Studies of sex hormone concentrations in nondepressed versus depressed women have produced inconsistent results. Estrogen may have a protective effect with regard to the risk for depression during menopause, but estrogen alone is not sufficient treatment for depression in menopausal women. Progesterone, another female hormone used with estrogen in many hormone replacement therapies for menopausal women, may actually diminish the antidepressant benefit of estrogen.

Depression is obviously far more than an emotional reaction to the trials of life. It does not indicate weakness of character, nor is it a lifestyle choice or a convenient excuse for failure to attain goals. Depression is a physical illness of body and brain. It not only affects our attitudes toward ourselves and our lives but also involves changes in how our bodies work.

5. Treatment

"I can't afford to wait to feel better. I've got to get back to work. I need help now!"

—A depressed psychiatrist

Treatment is available for most people suffering from depression, the most effective for moderate-to-severe cases generally being a combination of biological and nonbiological therapies. This usually means making use of both medication and psychotherapy.

The treatment of individuals with moderate-to-severe depression should include antidepressant medication unless such is specifically contraindicated by medical complications or by the unwillingness of depressed patients to accept medication or to self-administer them responsibly. Through the use of antidepressant medications selected to target the symptoms of depression and to produce minimal side effects, 80 percent of depressed patients can recover.

One key factor in the success of any antidepressant medication is the willingness of patients to take it as prescribed. Compliance with prescribed medications even in very responsible patients is rarely 100 percent. When patients have ambivalent or negative attitudes toward their medications, illness, or life situations, or toward themselves, medication compliance rates fall drastically, significantly impeding the chances of full recovery from depression. Psychotherapy can be essential in helping depressed patients identify attitudes and behaviors that cause problems in relationships and in circumstances of their lives (including the treatment situation) and in fostering the development of more beneficial responses. That may be the reason that studies involving various treatments for depression, both pharmacological and nonpharmacological, consistently show that patients treated with a combination of antidepressant medication and psychotherapy have the best recovery rates. The form of psychotherapy used appears to be less important as a predictor of successful treatment than the personality and skills of a well-trained, experienced therapist.

Psychotherapies

Psychotherapy is educational in nature and involves helping patients develop an understanding of various problems, as well as new beliefs and behaviors, which can ultimately lead to more successful adjustment. Psychotherapy can take many forms, but all involve a therapist working with an individual, or with a couple, a family, or a group of unrelated people.

Different kinds of psychotherapy have different primary goals. Psychotherapy may be supportive in nature or crisis-oriented. It may be designed to deal mainly with problem-solving in the here and now, or its aim may be to develop understanding, or insight, into the origins of the emotional discomfort. Psychotherapy may attempt to alter individuals' beliefs in order to change the way they perceive and interact with the world, or the objective may be to alter the way individuals recognize emotions and relate to others.

Psychoanalytic and Insight-Oriented Psychotherapies

Modern psychotherapy in this country came to prominence in the early half of the twentieth century with the teachings of Sigmund Freud and his followers. The original format was individual therapy several times weekly over a period of years. The form of therapy developed by Freud, known as psychoanalysis, involves delving into the individual's past relationships, emotional associations, and beliefs. It is based on Freud's theories regarding primitive instincts and the conflicts, usually unconscious, which arise from instinctual demands that must be suppressed or modified to allow the individual to adjust successfully. Freud theorized that the conflict between instincts, such as sexual (libidinal) drives, and the need to control them results in varying levels of anxiety and, at the extreme, emotional disturbances such as depression. This form of therapy analyzes the individual's instinctual drives, conflicts, anxieties, defense mechanisms used to cope with the drives and the anxiety, and patterns of close relationships. The premise is that developing insight will result in psychological growth and decreased symptoms. The underlying root causes of depression are thought to be loss and anger that have not been effectively managed and may not be consciously recognized.

Psychodynamic psychotherapy is a later derivative of psychoanalysis and shares many of the Freudian concepts and practices, but tends to be of shorter duration. Also referred to as insight-oriented psychotherapy, this form of treatment relies more on an understanding of the patterns of strong attachment to others displayed by individuals, especially as relates to problems in their lives. It also deals with defense mechanisms used to contain emotional discomfort. The belief is that once individuals become aware of the inner drives and conflicts that cause anxiety, anger, or despair, they can adjust their behavior to more effectively deal with those drives and thus relieve emotional discomfort. For example, through psychotherapy many depressed patients develop an awareness of previously unrecognized grief over the loss of a relationship, or a position, or something else that was important to them. They begin to understand the connection between their loss and the feelings of anger or rage that were deeply submerged beneath the guise of depression because of their inability to deal directly with the loss. Once these connections are made, depressed individuals often experience relief as they develop more beneficial responses and replace impotent rage with mastery over their dissipating anger.

Interpersonal Psychotherapies

Interpersonal psychotherapy was developed for the treatment of depression. Some of its more prominent advocates were Harry Stack Sullivan, Erich Fromm, Freida Fromm-Reichman, and Karen Horney. This form of psychotherapy focuses on interpersonal relationships and on improving relationship and communication skills as well as individual self-concept. The emphasis is on the here and now and on the specific problems that depressed people experience in the present. Interpersonal therapists are not as much interested in the developmental basis of depression in individuals as they are in how the individuals plan to deal with their present relationships and life circumstances. Coping with life's problems and the frequently resulting depression revolves around learning new adaptive behaviors to improve interpersonal and communication skills.

Interpersonal therapists tend to focus on four potential problems in the life experiences of depressed people: grief, interpersonal role disputes, role transitions, and interpersonal deficits. We instinctively understand that the devastation caused by grief can have a significant impact on our relationships with others and leave us vulnerable to depression. We accept that unresolved conflicts or constant disputes with others can be disruptive to our sense of well-being and lay the underpinnings for the development of mood problems. We may not be as aware that changes in our roles in life, even changes we identify as good, are a source of stress for most of us and can negatively affect our relationships with others, especially when the numbers of changes mount during a short period of time. Lastly, many of us tend to overestimate our "people skills" and do not recognize our own unpleasant behaviors, such as use of sarcasm, tendency to gossip, and the making of negative comments, including the belittling of others; yet such behaviors tend to distance people from us.

Cognitive Psychotherapies

Cognitive psychotherapy, commonly used in the treatment of depression, is advocated by prominent author-clinicians Aaron Beck, M.D., and his daughter, Judith Beck, Ph.D. (see "recommended reading" in appendix A for titles of their books). This form of psychotherapy operates on the premise that "we are what we think." It proposes that a person's tendency to have pessimistic thoughts and a negative worldview will result in depression.

Cognitive therapists work with patients to identify destructive myths, or cognitive distortions, i.e., strongly held beliefs that are distortions of reality. The groundwork for the distortions is usually laid in childhood, and many are culturally bound. Examples of common distortions include notions such as "grown men don't cry," "a lady doesn't lose her temper," "everyone must like me," and "if I'm good enough, he (or she) will love me."

The individual lives as if the distortions were reality and rarely questions their validity, even though the beliefs are often unrealistic and can lead to problems in daily life. Such issues arise during cognitive psychotherapy when the person seeks help for resulting problems with everyday living and relationships. Once the personal myths are exposed, therapists and patients work together to substitute more realistic concepts that result in long-term changes in the patients' attitudes, perceptions, and reactions to other people and to life.

A variant of cognitive psychotherapy is rational-emotive psychotherapy (RET), developed in the 1950s by an American, Albert Ellis, Ph.D. Ellis stressed that the RET therapist teaches clients to think straight, but does not think for them. In essence, this form of rational or cognitive therapy teaches clients to effectively analyze themselves. This view holds that human emotions do not magically arise from mysterious, largely unconscious needs and drives but develop directly from thoughts, ideas, and beliefs. In simple terms, human beings do not get upset by life events; we upset ourselves by irrational beliefs about life events and our relationship to them. Ellis emphasized that thinking is not always unemotional, just as emotion is not always unthinking. According to the tenets of RET, people are inclined to adapt to life events both emotionally and cognitively, but some individuals perceive, think, and then feel, while others perceive, feel, and then think.

One of the common practices of rational-emotive therapists is to identify irrational beliefs held by unhappy people and to encourage self-analysis so that these beliefs can be cast aside and replaced with more realistic ones. For example, many people hold the view that "if a thing is worth doing, it is worth doing well." This quotation is often used by perfectionists to explain their belief system. Unfortunately, they redefine that old saying to mean "if a thing is worth doing, it is worth doing perfectly." Since being perfect is impossible, this irrational belief often results in performance difficulties, frustration, and lowered self-esteem, all of which are frequently components of depression.

As its name implies, rational-emotive therapy encourages people to learn to think through their feelings and to analyze them in order to select for behaviors and emotions that contribute to successful living and emotional satisfaction.

Behavior Therapies

One form of individual therapy not often thought of as psychotherapy is behavior therapy, sometimes also referred to as behavior modification. Behavior therapy has always been heavily research-based and originated with behaviorist investigators Ivan Pavlov in Russia, B. F. Skinner in the United States, and Joseph Wolpe in South Africa and later the United States. Behavior therapy is practiced in many variations, but, at their most simplistic level, all involve identifying and measuring observable behaviors, not thoughts or feelings, and encouraging or extinguishing the target behaviors through the use of rewards (reinforcement) or punishment (aversive techniques) until new, more appropriate behaviors become ingrained through repetition and learning. Behavior therapy can be very effective with such problems as phobias and obsessive-compulsive disorders. It is less beneficial with mood disorders.

Biological Treatment of Depression

Before the advent of effective biological treatments for depression, a depressive episode often lasted eight months or longer. Electroshock (also known as electroconvulsive, or ECT) therapy was developed in the late 1930s and was the first effective treatment for severe depression. After the development of ECT, amphetamines were discovered and became the first medications capable of alleviating depression. They were widely used in the treatment of depression from the 1940s to the early 1960s. In the early 1950s, monoamine oxidase (MAO) inhibitors, discussed below, were accidently discovered to have antidepressant activities, and a biological revolution in the treatment of depression occurred. They drastically altered the outcome of depression, bringing significant improvement to more than 80 percent of sufferers and limiting the duration of episodes to approximately four months. Many of those early antidepressants are still in use today.

Most antidepressant medications require one to three weeks of a sustained dose for the development of a steady blood level. When the blood level stabilizes at a therapeutic, or effective, treatment level, depressive symptoms begin to decrease. The pattern of recovery is not one of immediate rebound; instead, people suffering depression experience an initial increase in energy level before they actually begin to feel better. Next comes an improvement in sleep and appetite patterns. At about the same time, a gradual lightening of mood begins.

The period of initial improvement, with its increased energy levels, is one of the most dangerous points in the cycle of depression. At that early stage in recovery, depressed people generally look better than they feel. Their posture becomes straighter, their walk brisker, and they are better at sustaining eye contact. While the people who know them well see the initial sparks of recovery, the depressed individuals themselves are unaware of improvement. They continue to feel despondent, hopeless, out of control. And therein lies a terrible irony. Before recovery begins, many who are suicidal cannot muster the energy to kill themselves. With the gradually increasing energy level that accompanies early recovery from depression, they become able to focus on the tragic task of suicide, not realizing that true relief is on the horizon.

The upward trend toward normal mood and function is not a smooth line. Progress is marked by good days and bad days, with a gradual tendency toward more good than bad and toward less severe, less frequent bad days until the mood finally smooths out somewhere near a normal level. Treatment of discrete depressive episodes may lead to rapid recovery but can take months to a year or more. Because there is currently no blood test for serum depression level, psychiatrists often recommend continuation of treatment with medication for nine months to a year after the return to normal mood in order to decrease the risk of relapse. Some people with chronic depressions require continuous treatment with antidepressant medication for years.

Individuals differ in their response to antidepressant medications, because they differ in the kind of drug-metabolizing enzymes their livers produce. The amount of medicine circulating in the blood (and therefore available to the brain) is determined to a large extent by how active and efficient liver enzymes are in breaking the medicine down. Individuals with liver disease or those with normally low levels of certain liver enzymes (which is determined by genes) cannot break down these medicines as quickly as other people. The advantage is that they require less medicine for the desired effect, so their pharmacy bills are less startling. On the other hand, they run the risk of being overmedicated by doctors prescribing normal adult doses of medicine so that they feel "drugged" or experience other unpleasant side effects and become reluctant to take antidepressants.

Before the early 1990s, women were excluded from most drug studies because of the complexity of the female hormone cycle and because of potential risks to the fetus if the woman became pregnant during the study. As a result, most of the research on current antidepressants was done with male subjects. For years, clinicians and researchers have known that more women than men take antidepressants, that women have proportionally more side effects than men, and that women receive less benefit from their medications. Researchers have now begun to study differences in how men and women metabolize medicines. They have found indications that young women's bodies may metabolize medicines differently from those of postmenopausal women, who more closely resemble their male counterparts in response to medications. What effect an understanding of female hormone interactions with medications will have on prescription patterns for women remains to be seen.

Another important issue in the treatment of depression is the use of polypharmacy. People commonly take multiple medications simultaneously to treat a variety of medical problems. Some medications are known to affect the way the liver and excretory organs handle medicines. Such effects on liver enzyme activity may reduce the effectiveness of an antidepressant or make it toxic by increasing its level (or the levels of its breakdown products) in the bloodstream. Antidepressants in turn may alter the ways in which other medicines, such as seizure medicines and contraceptives, are handled. Patients on medications for any illness should discuss with their physicians what impact an additional medicine may have.

All medicines, even the best of them, have side effects. Some fortunate people experience none of the side effects of antidepressants, while others struggle with adverse effects even at low doses. In some cases, the side effects can be relieved simply by lowering the dose of medicine or altering the time at which the medication is taken. For instance, most of the older antidepressants, such as Elavil and Sinequan, cause dry mouth and sedation. Since these are long-acting medications, they can be taken once a day so that the sedative effect can be turned into an advantage with bedtime dosing, which also delays the worst of the dry mouth condition until after the patient is asleep.

Antidepressants now in popular use fall into two obvious categories: the older ones and the newer ones.

Older Antidepressants

The older antidepressants are those developed between the mid-1950s and the mid-1980s. They generally fall into three categories: MAO inhibitors (MAOI), tricyclics (TCA), and miscellaneous.

MAO Inhibitors

The first effective medications for the treatment of depression worked by inhibiting the enzyme monoamine oxidase (MAO), which breaks down neurotransmitters important for maintaining normal mood. The development of these MAO inhibitors followed observations by astute clinicians that depressed tuberculosis (TB) patients became less depressed when treated with the antituberculosis medications that were available at that time. One of those antituberculosis medications provided the clue needed to develop MAO inhibitors (including Parnate and Nardil), the first line of antidepressants.

A serious side effect of those very useful antidepressants can occur when they are taken with certain other medicines (both prescription and over-the-counter preparations) or with certain foods. The result can be sudden and extreme high blood pressure, severe headache, and even strokes and death.

Two kinds of rare but potentially fatal interactions can occur when certain medications are taken with an MAO inhibitor. Medications such as over-the-counter cough syrups, diet pills, decongestants, asthma preparations, and many non-SSRI antidepressants can react with MAO inhibitors to stimulate excessive release of the neurotransmitters dopamine, epinephrine, and norepinephrine, which can cause dangerous blood pressure elevations.

The second type of harmful medication reaction can occur when MAO inhibitors are taken with medicines that increase serotonin release. The worst offenders are Demerol and the SSRIs (discussed below). Morphine and codeine, narcotics like Demerol, apparently do not cause the reaction. The toxic state caused by excessive serotonin levels can produce high fever, hypertension, and death (table 5.1).

Patients on MAO inhibitors are placed on a diet that eliminates certain foods such as aged cheeses, aged meats,

Table 5.1 Medication Restrictions for Monoamine Oxidase Inhibitors (MAOIs)

The following is a list of common medications that can cause severe hypertensive crises if taken by people on MAOIs. The list is not exhaustive. Individual variations in sensitivity to the reaction allow some people to use certain of the medications with caution; others will experience significant side effects. Patients should discuss medication restrictions with the physician prescribing the MAOI.

Avoid
    Stimulants, such as amphetamines and cocaine
    Decongestants, including over-the-counter preparations
    Antihypertensives (consult with physician)
    Antidepressants, such as tricyclics and SSRIs (consult with physician)
    Narcotics, especially Demerol (meperidine)

Use with caution
    General anesthetics
    Diet drugs
    Sedatives
    Hypoglycemics (consult with physician)

some vegetables, many preservatives, wines, and other alcoholic beverages (table 5.2). Those aged foods contain tyramine, which is normally broken down in the liver by monoamine oxidase enzymes. When individuals take MAO inhibitors, however, those enzymes are inactivated and thus prevented from breaking down tyramine, which then accumulates in the bloodstream in abnormally high levels that can increase blood pressure.

Because of their potentially dangerous side effects, MAO inhibitors are generally not used today as first-line treatments, but they remain useful as backups for the treatment of depression when other antidepressants fail. Patients on MAO inhibitors may wish to wear MedicAlert bracelets calling attention to these medications.

Tricyclic Antidepressants

Until the 1990s, the most frequently prescribed antidepressants included brand name medications such as Elavil, Tofranil, Sinequan, Pamelor, Anafranil, Norpramin, and Vivactil. These medications belong to a group known as "tricyclics" because of their three-ringed chemical structure (fig. 5.1). They are effective and generally inexpensive because of the availability of good generic preparations. Tricyclic antidepressants can be lethal in overdose, an unfortunate characteristic for medications used primarily in the treatment of a condition associated with high suicide risk.

Aggravating but nonlethal side effects of tricyclic medications include sedation, dry mouth, blurred vision, rapid heart rate, constipation, dizziness on standing quickly (due to sudden, transient drop in blood pressure), increased appetite, weight gain, and confusion. Of those, increased appetite with weight gain may be the most common reason women discontinue the medication even when it is effective in controlling their depression. More significant adverse effects are rarer, but may include abnormal heart rhythms with changes in the electrocardiogram (EKG), slightly increased risk for seizures in seizure patients, increased risk of falls in the elderly,

Table 5.2 Dietary Restrictions for Monoamine Oxidase Inhibitors (MAOIs)

The following is a list of common tyramine-containing foods that can cause severe hypertensive crises if ingested by people taking MAOIs. The list is not exhaustive. Because of individual variations in sensitivity to the reaction, some people can tolerate foods with small amounts of tyramine without problems; others will experience significant side effects. Patients should discuss dietary restrictions with the physician prescribing the MAOI.

High tyramine content (to be avoided)
Aged cheese, including Cheddar, Edam, Camembert, blue, Gouda, Swiss
Yeast products
Aged meats, processed meats, or any nonfresh meat, including sausage
Chicken liver or beef liver (more than two days old)
Sauerkraut
Pickled or salted herring
Licorice
Tap beer
Fava bean pods

Moderate tyramine content (to be used with caution)
Soy sauce
Sour cream
Cyclamates, monosodium glutamate

Low tyramine content (to be used in limited amounts)
Alcohol products, primarily those with color, such as beer, wine, and whiskey (colorless products such as vodka have very low tyramine content)
Pasteurized cheeses, cream cheese
Smoked fish, such as salmon, carp, whitefish
Caffeinated beverages, such as coffee, tea, soft drinks
Chocolate
Avocados (fresh)
Bananas
Raspberries
Oranges

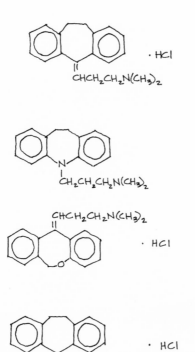

FIG. 5.I. Chemical structures of tricyclic antidepressants: (a) Elavil/amitriptyline, (b) Tofranil/imipramine, (c) Sinequan/doxepin, (d) Pamelor/nortriptyline.

and precipitation of mania in bipolar patients. Overdose on tricyclic medications may result in coma and death from abnormal heart rhythms.

Miscellaneous

The third group of "older" antidepressants includes medications that are not chemically related to each other (fig. 5.2). Most of them were never as popular as the tricyclics, although all are effective, and both Desyrel and Wellbutrin are increasingly used for treatment of problems other than depression. Desyrel (trazodone) is now most often used for nighttime sedation in conjunction with other antidepressants that may tend to

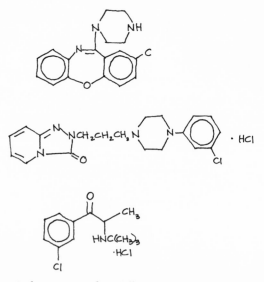

FIG. 5.2. Chemical structures of miscellaneous nontricyclic antidepressants: (a) Asendin/amoxapine, (b) Desyrel/trazodone, (c) Wellbutrin/buproprion.

be stimulating and therefore interfere with sleep. Asendin, a compound closely related to certain antipsychotic medications, unfortunately shares some troublesome neurological side effects of those medications; it is available, but not in common use. Wellbutrin continues to be used as an antidepressant, and is also prescribed for some adolescents with attention deficit problems. Recently it has been used for control of nicotine hunger in individuals in tobacco cessation programs (under the brand name Zyban).

Newer Antidepressants

For almost forty years, tricyclic antidepressants were the standard of care for serious depressive illnesses, yet the side effects of those medications made their use aggravating to almost all depressed patients and dangerous to many. Antidepressant use in the elderly, in suicidal patients, in people with liver disease, and in heart attack victims was a complicated issue. New weapons in the war against depression were overdue.

SSRIs

Beginning in the late 1980s, a new family of antidepressants became available, first in Europe and then in the United States. They were the selective serotonin reuptake inhibitors, better known as SSRIs (fig. 5.3). The SSRIs target the neurotransmitter serotonin, thought to be a primary agent in the development of depression. Serotonin is produced in nerve cells and released into the synaptic cleft between them, where it attaches to receptor sites on adjacent nerve cells, signaling cells to action. Approximately 80 percent of the neurotransmitter then is reabsorbed from the synaptic cleft back into the neuron and broken down or stored for later use. For reasons that are not clear, depression occurs when the brain functions as if it had insufficient amounts of serotonin in synaptic clefts. The SSRIs work by inhibiting the reuptake of serotonin from the synaptic cleft, resulting in increased amounts of the neurotransmitter being available to stimulate nerve cells, in contrast to MAO inhibitors that increase serotonin levels and norepinephrine levels by blocking their degradation by MAO enzymes.

The first of the SSRIs was the now-legendary Prozac, which was touted as a miracle drug by some clinicians and patients because of its effectiveness and relatively low rate of side effects, as well as its much lower lethal potential in overdose. Prozac was soon followed onto the market in the United States by Zoloft, Paxil, Luvox, and, most recently, Celexa. All are effective antidepressants and provide benefit in a growing number of other psychiatric conditions such as panic disorder and obsessive-compulsive disorder.

Another significant benefit is the improved safety profile of SSRIs as compared to previously available antidepressants. The SSRIs are safer for the elderly and for heart attack victims. In the treatment of depression, SSRIs have one other significant

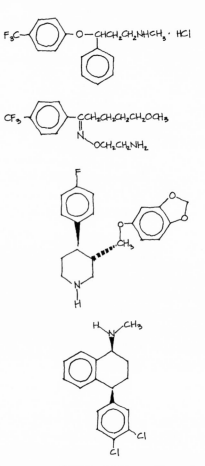

FIG. 5.3. Chemical structures of SSRIs: (a) Prozac/fluoxetine, (b) Luvox/ fluvoxamine, (c) Paxil/paroxetine. (d) Zoloft/sertraline.

advantage: they are less likely to be lethal in overdose than the older antidepressants.

SSRIs interact with many other medications by altering the speed or efficiency of liver enzymes that break down the other medications. In doing so, SSRIs can indirectly slow the breakdown of some medicines, such as the seizure medicine Tegretol and the blood thinner Coumadin, causing a buildup of those medicines in the bloodstream and resulting in significant side effects. It is wise to discuss with your physician any medication combinations that include an SSRI.

The most common side effects with this group of antidepressants are headaches, mild nausea, mild diarrhea, stomachaches, sleep disturbance, and interference with sexual orgasm. Except for the unfortunate tendency of the SSRIs to interfere with sexual performance or pleasure, side effects are infrequent and often gradually subside. The sexual side effects are not permanent and disappear with decreased doses or discontinuation of the medication. When the patient has experienced an otherwise good recovery from depression with an SSRI, the sexual side effects may be relieved by adjusting, changing, or adding medications to modify the sexual side effects. For example, adding the antidepressant Wellbutrin can reverse the sexual side effects of SSRIs in about one-third of cases.

When the SSRIs first became available on the U.S. market, they were highly sought as magic bullets for weight control, because those who take them tend to have diminished appetite, increased intestinal motility causing mild diarrhea, and weight loss during the initial phases of treatment. Unfortunately, that tendency reverses after weeks to months, and then appetite returns and weight increases.

Sleep disturbances can occur with SSRIs even when they are otherwise beneficial. The problem can sometimes be helped if the SSRI is taken in the morning rather than later in the day or if the dose is reduced. Another common tactic is to add a more sedating medication at night in combination with a morning dose of SSRI. Although some clinicians prescribe bedtime sedatives such as Ambien or Restoril, other clinicians try to avoid potentially habituating or addictive sedatives by adding a bedtime dose of one of the more sedating but nonaddictive antidepressants such as Sinequan or Desyrel.

Recent Additions
Four new antidepressant medications have been released in the United States in recent years. The latest, Celexa, is an SSRI. The other three—Effexor, Serzone, and Remeron—are

chemically unrelated to one another and are not SSRIs but share some of the benefits of SSRIs.

Effexor is the only antidepressant that inhibits the reuptake of serotonin, norepinephrine, and, to a lesser degree, dopamine, increasing the level of all three neurotransmitters in the synaptic cleft. Like the SSRIs, Effexor has a relatively low side effect profile, but at high doses can cause an increase in blood pressure, a potential cause for concern in hypertensive patients. As is the case with the SSRIs, overdoses with Effexor are unlikely to cause death, especially since one of the side effects of a significant overdose is nausea and vomiting.

Serzone is a new relation of the older antidepressant Desyrel, but appears to be more effective and less likely to cause sedation, sexual problems, and sudden, transient drops in blood pressure. Like the SSRIs, it acts on the serotonin system, but blocks some serotonin receptor sites in addition to inhibiting serotonin reuptake, utilizing two mechanisms to increase the amount of available serotonin in the synapse. It may be sedating and, because of its effect on liver enzymes, may cause serious side effects when taken with certain antiallergy preparations and with grapefruit juice. Serzone's potential advantage over other antidepressants may be a decreased likelihood to cause weight gain.

Remeron acts by increasing release of serotonin and norepinephrine (the two neurotransmitters most commonly associated with theories regarding the biological basis of depression) into the synaptic cleft, theoretically increasing the chance for successful control of depression. It is safe in overdose, has no blood pressure effects, and is a good bedtime sedative. It can cause increased appetite and weight gain, transient increases in drug-metabolizing liver enzymes, and transient, mild decreases in white blood cells (rare severe cases have been reported).

Other Medications for Depression

Treatment with current antidepressant medications is effective for 80 percent of depressed patients. When those medications are not effective, others may be added to increase the antidepressant effect. The medications that are frequently used to supplement antidepressants include stimulants, mood stabilizers, and hormone preparations.

Stimulants

The stimulant most commonly used as a second line of therapy for treatment-resistant depression is Ritalin, a medication used primarily in the treatment of narcolepsy (a condition of excessive daytime drowsiness) and attention deficit disorder. Ritalin is used occasionally as a primary medication (or as a second medication) for the treatment of depression in patients who are elderly, have conditions that prevent the use of common antidepressants, or have depressions that are chronic and poorly responsive to conventional antidepressants. While studies have shown benefit in the elderly apathetic patients treated with Ritalin, there is no evidence that Ritalin alone is effective for the treatment of moderate-to-severe depression. Clinicians use Ritalin cautiously because of its adverse effects: jitteriness, loss of appetite and weight, insomnia, irritability, headache, and especially abuse potential.

Other stimulants available by prescription in the United States include Dexedrin, Cylert, and Adderall. While all three medications can produce a mild, early, transient benefit in depression, there is no evidence that they are effective for moderate-to-severe depression. They share a similar side effect profile with Ritalin, including a high abuse potential.

Mood Stabilizers

Since the 1960s, bipolar mood disorders have been treated with mood stabilizers. The first such medication on the market was lithium carbonate (Eskalith Lithobid), a naturally occurring salt. For over twenty-five years, lithium has been the standard therapy for bipolar patients, effective in maintaining stable mood states and in helping to prevent acute episodes. During acute depressive episodes, bipolar patients often require the addition of an antidepressant, but this complicates the management of their illness, because antidepressant medications can precipitate manic episodes. In addition, recent studies suggest that use of antidepressants in bipolar patients may worsen the course of the illness by increasing the severity and frequency of mood swings.

Lithium was the wonder drug of its time, decreasing the misery of many bipolar patients by preventing or controlling mood swings, lessening the need for major tranquilizers, and decreasing the rate of hospitalization. Its benefits, however, come with a price. Lithium has a narrow safety range, so blood levels must be carefully watched. In overdose, lithium is toxic and can cause confusion, delirium, and death. Even at therapeutic doses, 75 percent of patients on long-term treatment with lithium experience side effects, including excessive thirst and urine production, hand tremors, excessive appetite and weight gain, nausea, diarrhea, suppression of thyroid hormone production, and decreased kidney function.

More recently, medications used for the prevention of seizures have begun to be prescribed for mood stabilization in bipolar patients who are lithium-resistant or who have conditions that prevent their use of lithium. The two anticonvulsants most commonly used for mood stabilization are Tegretol and Depakote. Both are metabolized by the normal liver, change the way liver enzymes break down other medications, can cause sedation, and must be monitored by blood tests. Depakote is likely to cause increased appetite and weight gain, particularly in women. It has also been reported to cause liver problems in rare instances, usually in children. Tegretol usually causes a transient, mild drop in the number of white blood cells, but occasionally it produces a severe deficiency of white blood cells requiring discontinuation of the drug. As is the case with lithium, neither Depakote nor Tegretol is a particularly effective antidepressant when used alone.

Several new medications (Neurontin, Lamictal, Topamax), now available in the United States for the treatment of seizures, are being tried also as mood stabilizers. They are presently used when other mood stabilizers are not effective or cannot be used. Neurontin is also used in the treatment of chronic pain disorders. Lamictal and Topamax have significant side effects, which may limit their use in mood swing disorders except in the most treatment-resistant mood disorders.

Hormone Preparations

Thyroid hormone supplementation (Synthroid, Cytomel) may be helpful in some depressed patients. Studies suggest that many treatment nonresponders may suffer from subclinical hypothyroidism and improve with the addition of thyroid hormone supplementation in addition to conventional antidepressant medication. Thyroid hormone supplementation alone, however, is not an effective treatment for depression unless the depression is solely the result of significant hypothyroidism. Patients with treatment-resistant depression who have minor shifts toward lowered thyroid function should be considered for thyroid hormone supplementation in addition to antidepressant medication. Treatment-resistant and rapid-cycling bipolar patients may have an increased incidence of thyroid dysfunction, and studies have shown enhanced mood stabilization in these patients when thyroid hormone supplementation is added. Some clinicians believe the benefit of thyroid hormone supplementation is especially likely to be effective in depressed women.

In menopausal and postmenopausal women, estrogen supplementation may have a protective effect against depression. It does eliminate many aggravating menopausal symptoms and enhances the sense of well-being in many women. Estrogen supplementation alone, however, is not sufficient treatment for depression in a woman who is menopausal because of aging or surgery. Progesterone, often a component of hormone replacement therapy for menopausal women, helps simulate a premenopausal hormone state. As discussed previously, progesterone can counter the mood-enhancing effects of estrogen. Some women believe that its use can precipitate an irritable depression, which is relieved only by discontinuation of the progesterone.

Electroshock Therapy

In the first half of the twentieth century, the only effective treatment for severe depression was shock treatment, which is accomplished by the inducing of a grand mal seizure in a patient through one of three means: electrical stimulation, use of insulin to drive the blood sugar to extremely low levels, or the administering of chemicals known to cause seizure. The only form of shock treatment now in common use (and also the safest) is electroshock treatment (also known as electroconvulsive treatment, or ECT). It has a relatively low

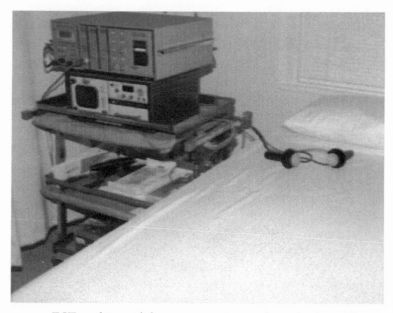

FIG. 5.4. ECT machine with heart monitor (picture by Richard Weddle; courtesy of Mississippi State Hospital).

risk of serious complications. Currently, electroshock treatment is performed while a patient is under general anesthesia and makes use of electrical stimulation to induce seizures (fig. 5.4). Although it sounds frightening, the amount of electrical stimulation administered to the head of a sleeping patient during electroshock treatment is less than that applied to the chest of a potentially conscious patient when emergency electrical cardioversion is necessary to correct a dangerous heart rhythm.

Effective control of depression generally requires a series of electroshock treatments given daily or, more commonly, two to three times weekly for a total of six to fifteen treatments. A major seizure appears to be necessary for an effective treatment, but the seizure need only occur within the brain itself. Convulsive movements of the body, such as jerking and straining, are not necessary for effective treatment. In fact, patients who are to receive shock treatment are placed under general anesthesia immediately before the treatment in order to prevent convulsive movements of the body. The procedure limits the chance of inadvertent injury to the body and minimizes distress to the patients. Despite graphic, negative portrayals of electroshock treatment in the popular media, modern techniques of electroshock therapy render the treatment relatively safe to the patient and do not alarm observers.

We do not know for certain why electroshock treatment works, but perhaps it is related to the massive release of neurotransmitters in the brain.

Electroshock treatment remains controversial in some sectors. Ironically, when properly administered to appropriately selected patients, it is the most effective, most rapid, and safest biological treatment available for severe depression. It is especially useful in patients who pose a high suicide risk and who may succeed in killing themselves before antidepressant medications have time to be effective, especially given the possibility that the patients would use those very antidepressants in lethal overdose.

Electroshock treatment is also a relatively safe alternative for other groups of depressed patients, such as patients who cannot tolerate medications because of serious medical conditions or women in the early stages of pregnancy when medications might cause abnormalities in fetal development. To the surprise of many, studies indicate that properly administered electroshock treatment during pregnancy may be safer for the fetus and the mother than antidepressant medications, even when the woman is in the last trimester of pregnancy. This is especially true in those severely depressed pregnant women who refuse all medications (including those needed to control dangerous medical problems such as hypertension and diabetes) or who refuse to eat and thus lose significant amounts of weight, which presumably results in fetal weight loss. Many elderly depressed patients show decreased sensitivity to conventional antidepressant medications but benefit greatly from electroshock therapy without serious side effects. As mentioned earlier, antidepressant medications taken by depressed bipolar patients can precipitate an acute manic episode or increase the frequency of mood swings. Many authorities therefore recommend that serious depression occurring in bipolar patients be treated with electroshock therapy rather than with antidepressant medications.

The most common side effects of properly administered electroshock treatment are headache, confusion, and memory disruption, all of which are temporary effects that resolve quickly and completely, according to most studies. The nightmare stories about shock treatment generally derived from the early history of the treatment when less-safe methods of seizure induction were used, when general anesthesia was not administered so that the body convulsed, and when the indications for treatment were much less selective.

Herbal Treatments

During the last decade, Americans have become increasingly interested in the potential benefits of alternative medicine, including herbal remedies. Those remedies, in use since ancient times, have been relegated to the realm of folklore by mainstream

Western medicine, although they continue to be used in many parts of the world. St. John's wort (*Hypericum perforatum*), an herb with yellow flowers, grows commonly in the wild. Its use as an herbal treatment has recently received widespread media attention. Extracts from St. John's wort are believed by many to be an effective treatment for some forms of depression. In fact, St. John's wort has been widely prescribed in Europe for many years for the treatment of milder forms of depression. There is as yet no conclusive scientific evidence of its effectiveness as an antidepressant or its risks and benefits in long-term use. In the United States, St. John's wort is sold in pill and liquid forms in health food stores and in pharmacies as a nutritional supplement and thus is not regulated by the U.S. Food and Drug Administration.

St. John's wort is not commonly recommended by medical doctors in the United States because of the lack of scientific evidence of its effectiveness. European studies of St. John's wort did find the herb to be useful in some cases of mild-to-moderate depression and to have fewer side effects than conventional antidepressant medications, but the studies generally did not meet rigorous scientific standards. The National Institute of Mental Health has now begun the first large-scale, controlled clinical trial in the United States to determine whether *Hypericum* has a significant antidepressant effect in patients with clinical depression.

Light Therapy

Seasonal affective disorder (SAD) is thought to occur in approximately 9 to 15 percent of people with recurrent depression and, as noted in chapter 2, is reportedly more common closer to the poles than nearer the equator. This unique form of depressive disorder is thought to be related to seasonal variations in length of daylight, which, of course, are more extreme near the earth's poles. Excessive sleeping and overeating during depressive episodes is thought to indicate a good chance for antidepressant response to light therapy.

Many clinicians in northern latitudes where SAD is more commonly diagnosed prescribe light for affected patients. Bright light therapy has been shown to suppress secretion of melatonin. Light therapy can be performed with either natural or artificial light.

People with mild seasonal mood variations often report feeling better on sunny days. For those individuals, exposure to direct sunshine, even for short periods of time, may be effective. Such individuals should arrange their living and working environments to take advantage of natural sunlight, choosing bright, sunlit houses and offices or work spaces with windows. When the weather allows, they should engage in outdoor activities for at least thirty to sixty minutes a day, preferably in the morning. The nature of the outdoor activities may range from vigorous participation in sports to coaching from the sidelines, from serious marathon running to casual ambling along wooded paths, or from weeding the garden to sitting in an outdoor swing reading about gardening. An hour's walk in the winter sunlight may be as effective as two and a half hours of exposure to bright artificial light. Some clinicians suggest that people with SAD make use of light banking to help prevent more significant depressive symptoms in the winter. Light banking consists of spending four or more hours a day in the sunlight for at least four days in a row just before mid-October.

For more severe seasonal depressions, daily use of artificial bright light therapy may be prescribed. Because natural sunlight is difficult to control, special lighting for houses of affected individuals may be recommended or a light box prescribed. The light boxes commonly used yield bright light (six thousand to ten thousand lux) from a bank of white florescent lights on a metal reflector with a translucent plastic diffusing shield. The device is mounted on a stand above a seated or reclining individual and tilted downward toward the head at an angle of 30 percent. Patients are instructed to focus on an illuminated area beneath the light source (where they can read) but not to look directly at the light. The exposure times prescribed generally range from thirty to ninety minutes daily, six to seven days a week. Morning light exposure, especially to bright light, may be more beneficial than afternoon exposure, although some individuals respond better to evening light exposure. Three to four weeks of light treatment may be needed for a patient to feel the effects.

Light therapy is popularly considered to be a relatively benign treatment, but it may have harmful effects. Many people exposed to light therapy complain of mild side effects such as headache, eyestrain, and "feeling wired." Another concern is that the intensities of light used in some regimens may be harmful to the retina over long-term use, so a preliminary ophthalmologic evaluation may be recommended before an individual starts this type of therapy.

Light therapy remains a controversial treatment method in standard Western medicine, but National Institute of Mental Health studies are promising.

Myths Regarding Depression and Its Treatment

Much of what passes for popular knowledge regarding depression can be consigned to the realm of myth. Some myths are relatively harmless; others have potential for contributing to the considerable risk associated with this potentially lethal illness.

Myth #1: You can talk yourself into or out of depression.

While our perspective on particular life events certainly affects our attitudes and contributes to our happiness or moodiness, these are transient feelings that are situational in nature and may indeed respond to a good inner "talking to." Clinical depression, however, is a physical illness that may not be caused by life circumstances and certainly does not respond to motivational lectures from ourselves or anyone else. Telling a severely depressed individual to "straighten up and pull yourself together" is about as useful and safe as telling a patient with severe congestive heart failure to take up power walking.

Myth #2: Depression will go away by itself, so treatment is not necessary.

It is true that many people experience time-limited depression from which they gradually recover without treatment. Often individuals do not recognize the nature of their problem until it has passed and therefore do not seek treatment. Relying on spontaneous remission is a potentially dangerous course for a seriously depressed individual to choose. At the very least, it results in unnecessary emotional distress, poor performance at school and work, and interference with close relationships for prolonged periods of time that may stretch from months up to two or more years. Then, of course, some depressed people never get better spontaneously because they do not live long enough to improve. Those unfortunate individuals gradually spiral into an increasingly severe form of depression that distorts their perceptions and beliefs and presents a bleak view of the future which often heralds self-destruction.

Myth #3: Once you are depressed, you never get over it.

Many people who experience significant depression have a time-limited illness that responds well to antidepressant therapy, so that they return to normal and are able to go on with their lives unimpeded. Others have episodes of depression separated by years of normal mood and behavior.

Myth #4: Depression is a sign of weakness of character.

No matter how many times this malignant belief is exposed for the ignorant myth that it is, there always seems to be need for yet another firm statement to the contrary. Depression is a physical illness in which measurable alterations occur in the brain and in other systems of the body. No one would dream of asserting that heart disease indicates a basic "lack of heart" and is a sign of cowardice. Legions of irate diabetics would rise up in anger if their disorder of the pancreas were labeled as evidence of the character flaw of gluttony. These obvious distortions are as absurd as the similar assertion that depression is caused by weakness of character.

Myth #5: People who talk about suicide do not do it.

This is a tragic misconception. Certainly there are many people who threaten self-destruction in moments of anger, intoxication, or fear who do not follow through once the immediate circumstances of their situation are resolved. However, depressed people who even hint of suicide or who allude to thoughts that they would be better off dead should be taken seriously. Eight of ten people who kill themselves have given definite clues as to their intentions, although some may be nonverbal and thus difficult to interpret.

Myth #6: Depressed people should not be asked about suicide, as it may put the thought into their heads.

Seriously depressed people almost universally consider suicide at some point despite their religious or philosophical convictions. Do not be afraid to ask about suicidal thoughts or intent. A particular response may point to the need for immediate action, and it is unlikely that a simple question about suicide will implant the idea for the first time in the mind of an individual with clinical depression. The more serious error would be to avoid asking the question when forewarning could literally mean the difference between life and death.

Myth #7: The most common method of suicide in men is self-inflicted gunshot wound; the most common methods in women are drug overdose and slitting of the wrists.

The preferred methods of suicide do vary according to sex, but the differences in chosen methods are no longer so disparate as was once the case. In the past, men did resort to quicker, more violent means of suicide, such as by gunshot, while women tended to select slower and less violent methods such as medication overdoses or carbon monoxide poisoning in the car. Recent indications are that the most common method of suicide for men and women alike is now self-inflicted gunshot wound.

Myth #8: Use of antidepressant medication is associated with loss of control and may result in self-destructive behavior or even homicide.

While the popular press has displayed a tendency in the past to exploit stories about extreme behavioral changes resulting from one or another of the newer antidepressants, the facts do not support those portrayals. People are at high risk for suicide during the earliest stages of recovery from depression when their energy level has picked up but they have not yet experienced an improvement in mood. The same phenomenon has been observed in the early-response phase of the use of all antidepressants. No one antidepressant increases the suicide risk more than another. As for homicidal impulses, there is no evidence that such behavior is associated with antidepressant medication.

Myth #9: Shock treatment is barbaric and causes permanent brain damage.

Despite the dramatic nature of this form of treatment and its stigmatization in popular movies and books, electroshock therapy has been shown in numerous clinical studies to induce faster remission from depression with fewer side effects than antidepressant medications. This is especially true in pregnant women, medically ill individuals, and the elderly. Although confusion and memory problems are common immediately following electroshock treatment, those side effects are temporary and disappear following completion of treatment. Studies once quoted as proving that electroshock treatment causes brain damage have fallen into disrepute as the methods used in the animal research have been reviewed and found to include procedures that were extreme, dangerous in themselves, and unlike methods used in human beings. Clinical research on electroshock therapy belies the myth that this type of treatment causes brain damage. Autopsies of the brains of people who received many courses of electroshock treatment over a period of years and later died of natural causes have been studied for obvious visible physical changes and for microscopic abnormalities. The studies fail to demonstrate evidence of brain damage related to those treatments. The only microscopic changes reported were those associated with normal aging. Most reports of permanent negative effects of appropriately administered electroshock treatments are highly subjective and difficult to substantiate although impossible to rule out entirely.

Myth #10: Children do not get depressed.

Unfortunately, children can suffer from depression, and some of them die by suicide. National Institute of Mental Health statistics for 1995 indicate that, while suicide is the third leading cause of death among young people fifteen to twenty-four years of age (yielding a suicide rate of 13.3 per 100,000), the suicide rate among children ten to fourteen years of age is 1.7 per 100,000. Methods chosen by young children include self-inflicted gunshot wound, drug overdose, and hanging.

6. Helping the Depressive

"Just tell me something I can do to help. I feel so helpless when I see him this way."

—The wife of a depressed man

How Can I Help Myself?

Depression is a thief that robs its victims of themselves, sometimes taking their lives in the process, yet depressed people are not completely at the mercy of their illness. They can help themselves.

The first critical step in recovery from depression is recognition that a problem exists, one that goes beyond a mere transient response to stress. The second critical step is to develop a willingness to seek help. If you suspect you are depressed, a call to your family physician should be your next step. The physician will assess your physical health and may choose to treat the depression at once or may refer you to a psychiatrist for evaluation and treatment. While the medical assessment and treatment are under way, there are things you can do to help yourself.

Self-Care Tip #1: Tend to your physical well-being.

Simplify your life. Set up a schedule of time for exercise and for regular sleep, seven to eight hours nightly. Whether or not you feel hungry, select a well-balanced diet and do not skip meals. By the same token, do not allow yourself to oversleep or overeat. Take a multiple vitamin daily. If you develop a significant change in your physical status, consult your physician without delay.

Self-Care Tip #2: Take all medications as prescribed.

Follow prescribed medical care attentively, making certain that you do not forget doses of medication. If you find that you are forgetful, as is often the case in depression, set up your medications in a container in daily portions a week ahead of time and keep the container in view where you cannot miss it. Handy, inexpensive, small plastic medication containers for this purpose are readily available at your local pharmacy or supermarket.

If your doctor recommends a course of antidepressant medication, inquire about the benefits and the potential side effects. Make certain you understand the instructions for taking the medicine, including which foods or other medicines you should avoid in combination with the antidepressant medication. Next, take the medication as prescribed. Antidepressant medication is guaranteed not to work when it is left sitting in the bottle. By the same token, do not make the mistake of thinking that if a little medicine helps a little, a lot of medicine will help even more. Rarely will you be correct, and when you are wrong the payback is not pleasant. If you experience problems you believe are related to the medication, call your doctor before discontinuing the medication.

Self-Care Tip #3: Do not add alcohol or recreational drugs to the mixture.

When your mind and body are depressed, they are having a difficult enough time maintaining some semblance of stability. Do not stress them further with alcohol, which itself has a depressant effect. Recreational drugs or someone else's medicine may also interfere with the activity of your prescribed medications.

Self-Care Tip #4: Do not allow your depression to socially isolate you.

Although you may feel uninterested in other people and their mundane conversations, push yourself to maintain contact with your family and close friends. They care about you and will be supportive of you even when you are not yourself.

Self-Care Tip #5: Avoid entertainment with depressive, self-destructive, or violent themes.

When you are depressed, thoughts and emotions that were never before part of your normal life come home to roost. As you attempt to survive and to overcome your illness, you have no need for messages of doom and gloom common to much of rock music and some country music. Choose instead music that you find soothing, energizing, or inspirational. Restrict your watching of television programs and movies to those with comedic or nonviolent, unemotional content. Be careful of the influences you allow into your head when you are most vulnerable.

Self-Care Tip #6: If you are considering suicide, contact your doctor at once.

People who make serious suicide attempts often retain some shred of hope that there is another answer even while they prepare for the ultimate tragic solution. In many, perhaps most, of us, there is an underlying core of strength that strives for mental and physical health. When you are seriously depressed, that impulse toward health may be deeply buried, but it will force itself through the fog at intervals. The awareness that you are suicidal and that this is not your normal train of thought is a signal from the healthy part of yourself of the need for a return to equilibrium. When your mood reverses and you return to your old self, you will think very differently from how you did when you were depressed, especially about something like the necessity for suicide. Give yourself a break. Call your doctor and explain why you are calling. Do not make him or her guess! Your life is in jeopardy, and this is one game you cannot afford to lose.

Self-Care Tip #7: Join a support group.

If you live in or near a metropolitan area, the chances are great that there will be one or more support groups for adults with depression. Although you may think that sharing your feelings and fears with other depressed people would be "depressing," give it a try. The understanding and pragmatic support you will receive will make your effort worthwhile. Perhaps more important, you will learn about your illness from people who have been where you are and survived. If your doctor is unable to refer you to a support group for depression, look in the yellow pages of the telephone book under mental health. You should find community mental health provider organizations and mental health consumer organizations listed there, including hot lines for use when you have an urgent need for emotional support (also see appendix A).

Self-Care Tip #8: Be circumspect when confiding information about your depression.

While the support of family and friends is an important component of your recovery, you are not duty bound to disclose details to casual acquaintances and colleagues. If you believe your depression is impairing your performance at work, you may choose to discuss your concern with your supervisor. Under the provisions of the Americans with Disabilities Act, you may be entitled to accommodations (such as flex time or a reduced schedule) to help you recuperate without your job being endangered. Do not discuss your depression in a job interview unless you feel the condition will be an issue in the interview process. It is probably best not to discuss your depression in a work-related environment, but if you must do so, discuss your strengths first and then comment simply on the temporary limitations you are experiencing and on what would help you perform well. Your personal life remains your own property, and it is your choice as to whether or not you disclose the details of your illness to anyone other than your doctor or therapist.

Self-Care Tip #9: Keep a journal.

Sometimes depressed people find that writing down what they are thinking each day helps to clarify ideas and to keep thoughts from spinning in circles of despair. Such a daily journal may be particularly helpful when you are climbing out from the deep pit of depression. Your mood will often vacillate from day to day during the early weeks of recovery. On an especially bad day when you think you have slipped back into the depths of despair, it often helps to read your journal entries from the preceding days where you can see recorded in your own words the early signs of improvement. You will remember hopefully that peaks and valleys are the rule at this stage of recovery, and your own journal will record your passage through them.

Self-Care Tip #10: Read, read, and read some more.

When you are depressed, your interest level and your energy level will almost certainly be low. Despite this, go to your local library or to your favorite bookstore. Find books to read: romances, westerns, histories, biographies, religious texts, philosophy, discussions of depression, inquiries into Area 51 and UFOs, anything that might hold your attention for a while. Your goal is to distract your mind from its depressive ruminations, not to impress other library patrons. Leave the tomes of Plato and Aristotle on the bookshelf; choose something easier to read. You may find relief in a "sappy" love story that ends well or in a tale of daring and bravado along the Oregon Trail. On the other hand, you may be more easily distracted by reading on unfamiliar topics. One woman's favorite topic was submarine warfare in the Pacific. She knew nothing about warfare or submarines and did not plan to remember anything she read, but curiously the subject held her attention while she sat in a recliner with her cat asleep in her lap.

Self-Care Tip #11: Use the computer with caution.

Although you may be able to divert yourself from your depressive thoughts by "surfing the 'net," do so in moderation. Many people have difficulty resisting the temptation to devote themselves exclusively to the computer for their recreation. Depressed people may be especially vulnerable to becoming obsessively focused on their computer, with a subsequent shutting down of interactions with their family and friends. It is easier in many ways to relate to a computer that asks little more from you than pecks on a keyboard or the barest movement of the mouse. Computers, however, cannot provide the kind of emotional and physical support that people do, although there may be an evolving role for support provided by family and friends via e-mail and by some on-line support groups when face-to-face contact is not available.

Self-Care Tip #12: Go outside into the sunlight for part of each day.

Fresh air and sunshine have a positive effect on most of us, depressed or not. Do not allow yourself to hide in a dark corner of your world. Seek the light both symbolically and literally. Remember that some forms of depression appear to be related to inadequate exposure to light.

Self-Care Tip #13: Do not allow yourself to lie in bed or on the couch all day.

Get up each morning, take a shower, eat some breakfast, and read the comic section of the newspaper. Do not allow yourself to burrow into the covers of your bed and hibernate.

Self-Care Tip #14: If you cannot sleep at night, get up.

When your nighttime sleep is disturbed by depression, do not lie in bed and stew. Get up. Drink a glass of milk and eat a sandwich or a piece of fruit. Do not grab a cup of coffee or a caffeinated soft drink. Read, watch television, or listen to music, so long as the subject matter is soothing and not stimulating. As soon as you feel sleepy again, go back to bed. If you fear that the act of walking from one room to another will kill the urge to sleep, then snooze in your recliner or on the couch. Sleep is sleep.

Self-Care Tip #15: Avoid major decisions while depressed.

Depression changes your perspective on yourself and on life. It distorts your patterns of thinking and may render your judgment faulty. Many people who unnecessarily make major decisions while depressed look back with regret, knowing that their judgment was adversely affected by their depression. When possible, it is usually a good idea to postpone major decisions while you are depressed, especially if those decisions are irreversible.

Self-Care Tip #16: Educate yourself about your illness.

One of the keys to regaining control of your life and your emotions is to gain a factual and realistic understanding of what has happened to you and to your body. Once you understand the beast, you have a much better chance of outmaneuvering it.

Self-Care Tip #17: Hold on to your personal faith.

If you have strong religious beliefs, hold on to them even when your illness is dragging you away. Depressed people have a tendency to lose their belief in themselves, in their future, in others, and in the idea that higher powers would care about insignificant humans such as themselves. If you previously had strong religious beliefs, act as if you still do. Sometimes you have to hold tightly to something to maintain your balance. Strong religious beliefs tend to exert a protective influence against suicide as well as to provide a bridge toward a much-needed social support system.

Self-Care Tip #18: If you are forgetful, write yourself notes.

Depression often interferes with memory, usually immediate recall and short-term memory. This is not a permanent affliction, but it can be embarrassing and aggravating. Do not try to remember everything. Carry a small notebook. Write yourself notes. Make lists. A depressed woman managed to maintain a reasonable level of productivity during the day by taping messages and "to do" lists for herself all over the house. Later, she measured her improvement by the decreasing number of notes on the refrigerator door, the kitchen cabinets, her dressing room mirror, and the inside of the front door. If you keep a list of tasks to be done, it is also a good idea to post the list of completed tasks where you can see it, so as to remind yourself that you have accomplished something.

Self-Care Tip #19: When you feel paralyzed by depression, take one step in some direction.

Depression can be, and often is, an overwhelming experience that can paralyze your ability to deal with circumstances and prevent your taking the necessary steps to reclaim your life. If psychological paralysis threatens, take one step in some direction so long as you can avoid an irreversible move. Even if it proves to be a step in the wrong direction, movement is positive, and the direction usually can be corrected with step two or three. Another way to accomplish this is to break large, complex problems down into single steps and then tackle them one at a time. As one depressed man commented, "The way to eat an elephant is one bite at a time."

Self-Care Tip #20: Do not blame yourself for being depressed.

Depression is an illness, not an item purposely selected off the menu of life. You will struggle against its manifestations, but it is unlikely that you will "snap out of it." The road back takes time and effort. Some days will be better than others. At times your energy for the fight against the beast will be lacking. The important thing is that you put yourself on the road to recovery, leaving the beast behind you while giving yourself a rest break every now and then.

How Can I Help Someone I Love Who Is Depressed?

Watching a friend or someone you love in the throes of depression is a frightening prospect. You feel unsettled and helpless. The person you see is in many ways different from the person you thought you knew. You want your loved one back. There are a number of things you can do to help someone in this condition.

Caring Tip #1: Express empathy and concern.

People who are depressed often become self-absorbed, withdrawn, and uncommunicative. Explaining themselves takes too much energy, and they have little to spare. Encourage short conversations, but avoid long talks. If you try to probe their thoughts and feelings by playing "twenty questions," they will often shut down and communicate little. Instead, express your concern and your awareness of the pain and hopelessness they feel without implying that you truly comprehend their devastating experience. That would be presumptuous. You do not understand depression until you have lived through it. You can, however, provide loving support to help pierce the emptiness felt by your loved one.

Caring Tip #2: Avoid saying, "Snap out of it!"

No matter how difficult life with a depressed person is for you, it is more difficult for your loved one. A curt "Snap out of it!" or "Just pull yourself up by your bootstraps!" reflects simplistic thinking in the face of the reality of depression. You might as well tell a quadriplegic to get out of bed and walk!

Caring Tip #3: Avoid giving advice unless it is requested.

When someone you care about is depressed, your natural inclination will be to take a problem-solving role. You may cast about for the cause of the problem and be tempted to give advice on how to take care of it. It may seem perfectly obvious to you that your friend could be much happier if she would just leave her womanizing husband or that he would be more self-confident if his wife did not criticize him constantly. Hold your tongue. Be supportive and empathetic. Try to give your loved one hope. Leave your adviser role at the door unless you are asked for help. If your advice is solicited, proceed cautiously with simple suggestions. Discourage major decisions and irreversible moves when possible.

One exception to this general injunction is that you must act in the best interest of your loved one if you believe suicide is an imminent risk.

Caring Tip #4: Instill reality and minimize guilt.

Depressed people often magnify their transgressions. The depressed father becomes convinced that his job performance is so inadequate that he will be fired, thus robbing his teenagers of their chance to go to college and destroying their hopes for success. The depressed older woman may believe that she presents an undue financial burden to her children. A depressed child may be convinced that his parents are divorcing because of him. If these exaggerated beliefs are present, you should act with patience and consistency in reassuring the depressed person of his or her worth and competence. Although you may find expressing deep and sincere emotions awkward, it is especially important to convey in clear and heartfelt words the true value the depressed person has to you and to others.

Caring Tip #5: Take the time to notice changes in behavior.

Changes in behavior in a severely depressed person may be either signals of improvement or harbingers of deterioration, perhaps even suicide. A sudden apparent improvement in mood following an extended period of despair is not necessarily a good sign. People who have finally decided to commit suicide often feel a temporary relief and appear improved. Monitor your loved one's behavior. When changes occur, be especially vigilant in looking for additional signs that may indicate the direction of the change.

Caring Tip #6: Encourage healthy behavior and support treatment efforts.

Do not nag. Be supportive. When the opportunity arises, encourage your depressed loved one to seek professional help. Discuss frankly the fear of being stigmatized. Provide reassurance of your love and support. Encourage activities that promote emotional health, such as light exercise and proper diet. When your loved one is ready to accept professional help, assist in making the arrangements and accompany the person to the first appointment. Then help follow through with the plan of treatment.

Caring Tip #7: Be the better part of yourself.

In communicating with your loved one, keep your best face forward. Use light humor to defuse tension between the two of you, making certain the humor is not directed against the depressed person. Laugh good-heartedly at yourself or share a humorous observation. If your wit has a tendency to include sarcasm, squelch it. The healing gift of laughter is not born of sarcasm. When the tension cannot be defused, do not yell or shout. Depressed people and their distorted perceptions can be frustrating to those who care for them, provoking bouts of impotent anger. Avoid name-calling or rehashing old battles. Maintain a calm demeanor or excuse yourself gracefully and unobtrusively. You need not be a saint. You can go for a drive alone and utter every curse word you know until you feel better. Just do not do so in front of the depressed person you love. Above all, respect the confidential nature of your relationship and do not gossip behind your loved one's back.

Caring Tip #8: Keep your head.

If your loved one's depression has dropped unaccustomed responsibilities into your lap, think. Do not emote. Sometimes the one who becomes depressed is the one in the relationship who formerly handled the business and made the big decisions. The depression may have robbed this person of the ability and self-confidence to carry out those tasks and saddled him or her with unreasonable doubts and fears. You may never before have filled out the income tax forms or taken a loan from the bank, but with a little self-education and tolerance for some level of anxiety, you will find that business matters can be managed and decisions made.

Caring Tip #9: Be realistic about your own expectations of yourself.

No matter how much you want to, you cannot banish depression (your own or anyone else's) by sheer effort of will. No matter how much love you express, you cannot entirely fill the vacuum the depressed person feels. No matter how vigilant you are, you cannot always prevent the suicide of someone who is determined to die. Your role is to be loving and patient, to maintain the household routine as much as possible, and to be supportive of efforts to comply with professional help. Do not blame yourself for your loved one's depression. By the same token, do not interpret that depression as evidence that you are not as loving or as nurturing as you should be. You do not have that much control over your loved one's emotions.

Caring Tip #10: Seek help for yourself.

Loving someone who is depressed is a stressful experience. The deeper your love is for that individual, the more likely you will be to experience a form of secondhand depression. It may not be as debilitating as the depression your loved one lives with, but the experience does shake your view of yourself and your relationship. You may experience anxiety, occasional tearfulness or irritability, and changes in your own sleep and appetite patterns. You may worry a lot and often feel off-balance. You probably do not need antidepressant medication yourself, although in some circumstances you may. You do need to talk with someone you trust, to express your fears and your frustrations, and to get an occasional reality check. Choose a close friend or relative with common sense, see a minister, or join a support group. If your own depression becomes more severe, get professional help. Do not forget to help yourself while you try to help your loved one.

When Is Involuntary Treatment Needed?

In the best of all worlds, depression would not exist, or, if it did, everyone who became depressed would seek professional treatment immediately. Unfortunately, neither proposition is true. For some, the beast of depression is too overwhelming, too black, too shameful, too unbeatable to allow for hope or for help.

When depression is too severe to allow the sufferer to recognize the reality and to accept help, and especially when suicide seems a likely prospect, involuntary treatment is recommended. Involuntary treatment requires legal intervention in most states in order to ensure that the rights and wishes of the depressed individual are considered as well as the severity of the depressive illness. A core issue is the question of whether there is immediate likelihood that the depressed individual will harm him- or herself or others as a result of the illness. Although procedures for consideration of involuntary treatment vary from state to state, most involve an assessment of the depressed person by one or more physicians or psychologists who provide a report to the judge or judge's designee. Some states allow physicians to hold depressed patients in a hospital against their will on an emergency and time-limited basis (usually no more than twenty-four to seventy-two hours) while legal proceedings are instituted. The final decision as to whether an unwilling patient will be treated involuntarily rests with the judge who determines whether such care is necessary and, if so, where the person will be treated. Court orders for treatment are time-limited and often detail specifications for treatment such as naming the hospital where the treatment will occur and the conditions surrounding use of medications. If you suspect that involuntary treatment may be needed, contact a psychiatrist or a local mental health service for information about the procedures in your area.

The decision to pursue involuntary treatment for a loved one is a difficult one to make. You will seek to avoid that avenue unless it is absolutely necessary. Your fears can be legion: the fear of eternally alienating your loved one, the fear of overestimating or of underestimating the problem, the fear of the cost or the stigma. The fact is that when your loved one's continued existence is in question, you may be forced to express your love by securing the help needed whether the person is willing or not. In the worst of these circumstances, your gift of love may be to fight for your loved one's survival even at the risk of damaging the relationship. As English poet Andrew Marvell wrote, "The grave's a fine and private place, / But none, I think, do there embrace."

7. Searching for a Cure

"This makes me even more determined to find an answer."
—A research scientist to the grieving parent
of a teenage suicide victim

Knowledge of the genetics, anatomy, and chemistry of depression has mushroomed over the past fifty years through research funded by private as well as public sources. Along the way, basic research was translated into the production of effective antidepressant medications. For example, the selective serotonin reuptake inhibitors (SSRIs) are "designer" drugs developed as a result of data pointing to low levels of serotonin as a cause for depression.

As effective as current antidepressants are, they work in only about 80 to 85 percent of depressives. They also take a month or more to relieve symptoms, leaving a potentially fatal window of opportunity for self-destruction. Even when effective, current medicines for depression can cause unpleasant, sometimes serious, side effects. New methods of treatment are needed and will come from research under way in major medical centers around the world.

As we have seen, research indicates that depression is a complex phenomenon. It is not surprising, then, that researchers on the trail of the causes and of ways to treat and prevent depression pick up and investigate different clues in their efforts toward a common goal—the discovery of the roots of depression. Much of the research is, of course, focused on the "hard" sciences: the biology, chemistry, physiology, and anatomy of depression. Some investigators, however, are intrigued by human experiences more difficult to measure: the psychology of depression, the interplay of personality and mood, the effects of stress, the influence of family and community relationships, and the impact of environment. Like the blind wise men studying the elephant from trunk to legs to tail, those doing research on depression all study pieces of the same beast, and one day, through their diverse efforts, the full image of depression will be revealed.

In 1993, the Human Brain Project was announced by the United States National Institutes of Health, the parent agency of the National Institute of Mental Health. The Human Brain Project is a broad-based, long-term research initiative founded to support research and development of advanced systems and technologies for use by neuroscientists and behavioral scientists.

Research on depression goes on worldwide. In the United States, research is under way at the National Institute of Mental Health and at major medical centers affiliated with academic facilities. The research tends to fall into broad, overlapping categories: biological, psychological, and environmental. Within each of those categories, some research is groundbreaking, while the rest seeks to refine knowledge previously gained.

Most basic research today focuses on biological factors, which follows from the hypothesis that some individuals are "hardwired" for depression, that their anatomy and chemistry (resulting largely from hereditary factors) preordain a tendency toward mood disorders. Not all investigators, however, are convinced that predisposition to depression is primarily a result of abnormal anatomy and chemistry.

Environmental Factors

Bright Light

As discussed in chapter 2, humans have long attributed mood-altering potential to various weather and climatic changes.

We speak of "winter blahs" and "spring fever." Rainy days "make" some people feel listless or "blue," while others feel peaceful, cozy, and relaxed. Summer days may be energizing or just hot and dusty, depending on the personal preference of the individual. For some, autumn is the favorite season of the year, while for others it is a time of moodiness. Why? Why are there such differences among individuals? Are the attitudes learned or the result of an inborn template? Do weather and climate factors really effect mood? If so, in what way? The connection between dark winter days and serotonin depletion in depression is a tortuous one, based on circumstantial evidence and doubted by some well-established researchers.

When Norman Blumenthal and his team began their research, funded by the National Institute of Mental Health, on seasonal affective disorder (SAD) in 1984, they focused on a relationship between mood and winter darkness originally noted by laypeople living in northern climates such as Alaska, northern Canada, Scandinavia, and Siberia. The notion of SAD as a distinct mood disorder remains controversial in some quarters, and its primary treatment—light therapy—is viewed with disdain because it is not "molecular enough," according to Anna Wirz-Justice from the Chronobiology and Sleep Laboratory of the Psychiatric University Clinic in Basel, Switzerland. Supporters of light therapy believe that the simplicity of the treatment makes it suspect to researchers accustomed to dealing with the complexities of human physiology.

The idea for light therapy developed from research on mammals and their responses to seasonal changes, responses that include changes in sleep, eating behavior, and weight (resulting from changes in activity level and appetite). A circadian pacemaker in animals, located in the brain, detects changes in duration and intensity of light and signals glands to alter the activity levels of body functions in order to adapt to seasonal changes. Since humans retain some functions of that circadian pacemaker, a logical connection was made between winter depression and changes in day length. That bit of logic resulted in fifteen years of SAD research, not only in northern climes, but also in the extreme southern hemisphere, with its inverse winter season, as well as in sunny countries such as Italy, India, and Japan.

The data reported from three U.S.-based projects and from worldwide research indicates that SAD may be a distinct subtype of depression and that the benefits of light treatment for SAD are not mere placebo effects, but may actually be superior to treatment with antidepressant medications.

A study by Michael Terman and colleagues at Columbia University and the New York State Psychiatric Institute, by Charmane Eastman and colleagues from the Biological Rhythms Research Laboratory at Rush-Presbyterian-St. Luke's Medical Center in Chicago, and by Alfred J. Lewy from the Sleep and Mood Disorders Laboratory at the Oregon Health Sciences University in Portland points to the effectiveness of treatment with bright light therapy, from 0.5 to 1.5 hours each morning six to seven days a week for at least three weeks.

Dr. Lewy postulates that SAD is caused by a phase-shift. That is, most patients with SAD develop a phase-delay, or a slowing of their internal biological clock (circadian rhythm), in the wintertime, leading to alterations in neurotransmitter balance and melatonin production and resulting in lethargy and the development of winter depression. The phase-delay is reversed in SAD patients who respond well to morning light treatments.

What is the light-sensitive organ in humans with regard to the internal biological clock and seasonal affective changes? Most research has focused on the retina of the eye, but there is speculation that other tissues may also be light sensitive. A recent study at Cornell University School of Medicine shows that light can affect the body clock through the skin as well as through the retina. Dan A. Oren of Yale University hypothesizes that blood serves as the "messenger" for light. Dr. Oren and his team at Yale University's Center for Light and Psychiatry are looking at how light effects the hemoglobin in red blood cells in SAD patients and in healthy individuals. Dr. Oren believes that blood absorbs light through the skin and the eyes and travels to the pituitary gland and the inner brain structures that form the biological clock where the "message" is relayed. He speculates that SAD may be a blood rather than a brain disorder and that the defect may be the inability of blood to absorb sufficient light energy.

High-Density Negative Air Ionization

The air around us is filled with molecules that can be electrically charged (positive or negative) or neutral. The charged particles, called ions, are formed when energy acts upon a molecule (such as carbon dioxide, oxygen, water, and nitrogen found in the air) to eject a small, negatively charged particle called an electron, thus creating a positively charged ion. The ejected electron attaches to a nearby molecule, which becomes a negative ion.

Billions of negative air ions are created daily by air friction, lightning, cosmic rays, radioactive elements in the soil, ultraviolet radiation, storms, winds, waterfalls, and vegetation such as evergreens and ferns. The concentration, or density, of negative ions in the air varies depending on the nature of the environment in an area. For instance, fresh air over a grassy field in the country contains an approximately equal number of positively and negatively charged ions. A cubic centimeter (about the size of a sugar cube) of such air may contain two thousand to four thousand negative ions, while the same amount of air collected near Yosemite Falls will yield over a hundred thousand negatively charged ions. On the other hand, the density of negative ions in the air may be less than one hundred per cubic centimeter over a busy freeway during rush hour.

With each breath of air, we pull positive and negative ions into our bodies, transferring the ions via our blood from the lungs to all body cells. Some researchers believe that air ions absorbed into our body cells can affect the function of the cells, causing subtle changes in the way our bodies work depending on whether the ions are predominately positively or negatively charged.

The first hint that air ionization could affect humans came in 1932 as the result of a chance observation by C. W. Hansell, a research fellow at RCA laboratories and an international authority on ionization. He observed a fellow RCA scientist who exhibited significant mood swings while working beside an electrostatic generator. Hansell studied the phenomenon and found that the scientist's irritable, depressed moods occurred on days when the electrostatic generator produced positive ions, while more lighthearted moods occurred when the machine generated negative air ionization. His observation was confirmed months later by European research.

Research on air ionization began in the 1950s when Dr. Albert Kreuger, professor emeritus of the University of California at Berkeley, and Dr. Felix Sulman, professor of pharmacology at the Hebrew University in Israel, discovered that positively charged ions stimulate the production of the neurotransmitter serotonin, whereas negative ions decrease the serotonin level. Sulman demonstrated three effects of positive ion excess: irritation and tension, exhaustion, and hyperthyroid response. These conditions, along with symptoms of depression, anxiety, headaches, and low-energy physical and mental functions, were found to be alleviated by an increased negative ion count in the air.

If SSRIs were designed to relieve depression by increasing the concentration of serotonin at the neuronal synapses, how could negative air ionization provide the same benefit by decreasing the serotonin level? We do not know. Studies indicate that increased serotonin stimulates the release of epinephrine (better known as adrenalin), which allows the body to deal more effectively with stress. Some proponents of negative air ionization believe that depletion of epinephrine is caused by prolonged exposure to high serotonin levels, thereby diminishing the body's defense against stresses, including the negative effects of positive air ionization.

Recent research indicates that negative ions in the bloodstream increase the delivery of oxygen to cells and tissues and can cause the same exhilaration produced by a few deep breaths of pure oxygen. Positive ions, on the other hand, slow down the delivery of oxygen, causing symptoms similar to those seen in oxygen starvation. Negative ions also appear to stimulate the reticulo-endothelial system, one of our body's defenses against disease. Preliminary research suggests that negative air ionization is of benefit in the treatment of pain, burns, and smoking-induced lung disease, as well as depression.

Although the method by which air ionization works to relieve depression is unknown, an increasing body of research confirms its effectiveness, especially at higher ion concentrations. The previously mentioned study by Michael Terman and colleagues on bright light therapy also revealed an unexpected beneficial effect of high density negative air ionization in the treatment of seasonal depression. With a series of brief daily exposures to air ionization, the volunteers experienced greater than 50 percent symptom remission rates (especially when the treatment was extended beyond two weeks) with no side effects. Further research is needed to validate the benefits and the safety of high density negative air ionization treatment for depression.

Electromagnetic Fields

Studies funded by the National Institute of Mental Health are under way to review the effect of electromagnetic fields on various body functions including brain activity. Transcranial magnetic stimulation (TMS) is one such area of research. TMS was developed by neurologists ten years ago to study motor systems in the brain. It involves the use of a small but very powerful handheld electromagnet, similar to the electromagnets in MRI scanners. The magnet is held at the side of the head on the scalp and turned on and off, creating a strong magnetic field that passes through the skull. The rapidly changing magnetic field causes an electrical current in nerve cells of the brain, exciting them to fire. The location of the magnet against the head theoretically causes activation of specific sets of nerves adjacent to the magnet. Thus, if the magnet is held over the right ear, the left thumb may reflexively move (the right brain controls the left side of the body). TMS may allow us to safely and painlessly map the parts of the brain involved in different functions, including emotions.

Recent studies by Mark S. George and colleagues at the Medical University of South Carolina have shown that TMS placed over the frontal lobes of the brain may cause subtle changes in mood in healthy adults, depending on whether the right brain or the left brain is stimulated (right causes happiness, left causes sadness). This remarkable finding has been confirmed by two double-blind studies (i.e., research projects in which neither the evaluator nor the research subject knew whether the implement used was a true magnet or an inert fake). How the electromagnetic force field affects mood is not known, but some researchers speculate that TMS may work in a manner similar to that of electroshock treatment (ECT), the mechanism of which is also unknown. If research establishes the effectiveness of TMS as a treatment for depression, the next step will be to compare its safety and effectiveness against both antidepressant medications and ECT.

Psychological Factors

Research looking at the effects of environment on the development of depression is based on long-held observations that mood alterations often follow significant life changes. Such research is difficult to design along strict scientific lines, because it deals with abstract concepts not easily measured or controlled. Current research, for example, includes studies on relationships and stresses—phenomena for which there are few scientific measures.

Could changing gender roles be increasing the rate of depression among men? Polash M. Shakahan and Jonathan T. O.

Cavanagh of the Royal Edinburgh Hospital in Edinburgh, Scotland, studied hospital records from 1980 to 1995 and found that the number of men admitted for depression rose during that time, while the number of women admitted for depression decreased. The investigators noted that the trend coincided with a major shift in social roles in Scotland. They suspect a link between rising levels of male depression and the social and economic advances made by women. Another interpretation of their data is that men have become more comfortable seeking help.

Many questions remain regarding the effects of environment on mood. What is the long-term effect of early childhood deprivation? Are children who lose a parent early in life at greater risk for developing depression later? Is a single-parent family a risk factor? Can a single severe stress lead to depression, or is the cause a series of small stresses? Are stay-at-home mothers at higher risk for depression than mothers who work outside the home? Do rapid social changes increase risk?

Personality Traits

Personality traits appear to have a strong influence on the course and outcome of mood disorders, but study results are controversial and difficult to replicate. Preliminary results of studies to identify specific personality traits that affect the outcome of unipolar depression and bipolar disorder suggest that introversion has a negative effect on the course of depression, while extraversion has a positive influence. "Neurotic" individuals (people with chronic mild forms of depression, anxiety, hypochondriasis, self-esteem problems) have a more troubled course if they have bipolar disorder, but not if they have unipolar depression.

At the University Department of Psychiatry, Hôpital Pinel in Amiens, France, G. Loas and colleagues are looking at the relationship between dependency and depression. Although previous research had found a significant positive relationship between dependency and the level of depression, when the Loas team studied a sample of 202 university students, they found almost no consistent relationship between dependency and depression. The contradictory results indicate that further research is needed.

Investigators are also looking into the relationship between attitude and problem-solving styles and depression. Are there certain personality types that are predisposed to depression? Do people who swallow their anger and demand of themselves a measured response to provocation run a greater risk for developing depression? Are specific problem-solving styles found more commonly in people who suffer depression?

Defense Mechanisms

At the University of Oslo in Norway, P. Hoglend and colleagues are investigating the predictive value of psychological defenses on the outcome of depression. Because certain defenses are commonly found in patients with major depression, the researchers are looking at the predictive value of those defense mechanisms on the course of depression. Earlier studies indicated that self-observation—a highly adaptive defense—is commonly found in individuals who improve more than predicted by their initial status. Preliminary results found by the research team in Norway support the theory of a hierarchy of defenses affecting the course of depression. Further research will examine such defense mechanisms as passive-aggressiveness, acting out, help-rejecting complaining, identification, projection, and devaluation in relation to the onset, course, and treatment response of depressive disorders.

Stress Response

One National Institute of Mental Health study is looking at stress factors that potentially relate to suicidal ideation, including life stress, the patient's perception of stress, social support, personality, alcohol use, chronic conditions, distress symptoms, and sociodemographic background. Using data from a health survey of adults in Reykjavík, Iceland, researchers found that financial hardship, legal problems, family difficulties, stress perceptions, and low material support are significantly related to thoughts of committing suicide. Chronic conditions, such as frequent use of alcohol and emotional distress (depression, anxiety, hopelessness, pain), are also related to suicidal ideation. In addition, low self-esteem and low sense of mastery are both associated with suicidal thoughts. No significant relationships were found between sociodemographic background and suicidal ideation.

Few studies have focused on a person's thoughts of his or her own suicide or suicide planning, despite the realization that ideation and planning are important steps in the process of suicide, a process characterized by a stepwise hierarchy of actions of increasing significance. Such research can lead to better predictive measures and, it is hoped, limit the number of deaths due to suicide.

A. Bifulco and colleagues at the Socio-Medical Research Centre, Royal Holloway, University of London, are engaged in a study to confirm an earlier finding that approximately 40 percent of women who experience a severe life event and also have two ongoing psychosocial vulnerability factors (few close relationships and low self-esteem) will develop a major depression. Initial results indicated that 37 percent of the vulnerable women became depressed during the study period. The majority of the women in the study experienced a severe life event, and 48 percent of them experienced onset of depression. Contrary to the researchers' expectations, the presence of one vulnerability factor was almost as great a risk as the presence of both factors.

Religious Beliefs

One of the most interesting new avenues of research is the relationship between health and religious faith. In recent years, studies have emerged that suggest a relationship between health maintenance, recovery from serious illness, and deep religious faith. Such studies are understandably difficult to design along established scientific principles, but increasing data suggests the presence of a significant correlation. For instance, a recent study at Duke University indicated that the stronger a person's religious faith is, the more quickly the person will recover from depression, especially if the individual is disabled or chronically ill.

Biological Factors

Most of the current research on depression deals with biological aspects of the illness and is focused on an array of biological approaches, from studies of abnormalities in structure, chemistry, development, and communication systems of the brain to studies of the responses of human subjects to medications. In the latter case, much of the research involves attempts to refine our current treatment approaches rather than to break new ground. For instance, many studies currently funded by the National Institute of Mental Health compare the relative benefits and disadvantages of commonly used antidepressant medications. The studies are conducted with volunteers who meet the diagnostic criteria for one of the forms of depression and usually compare a newer antidepressant medication to an older, established antidepressant, allowing researchers and clinicians to distinguish the relative value of the newer medication as a tool against depression. At the present time, studies utilizing depressed human volunteers are comparing the effectiveness of the newer antidepressants (the SSRIs, Wellbutrin, Serzone, and Effexor) to one another and to the older antidepressants, most of which belong to the tricyclic class (TCA)—e.g., Tofranil, Elavil.

The clinical research that results directly in improved diagnosis and treatment of depression usually follows from more basic research into the anatomy, chemistry, and genetics of depression. The more basic research generally follows one of four models: brain imaging in living people, post mortem examination of human brain tissue, examination of living human tissue, and animal studies.

Recent studies of both living and post mortem brain tissue point to the importance of two brain regions in the development of depression: the frontal lobes and the hypothalamic-pituitary-adrenal (HPA) axis. Both areas are interconnected with the limbic system.

Brain Imaging

Brain imaging research relies on several advanced scanning techniques—MRI, ƒMRI, PET, and SPECT. As discussed in chapter 4, MRIs provide excellent anatomic images of brain structures at various levels, but do not provide evidence of brain activity. PET and SPECT scans provide images that allow comparison of activity in different areas of the brain but require the injection of a short-lived, mildly radioactive organic material, thus limiting their value in repeated studies on human volunteers. An ƒMRI produces images of activity levels in various areas of the brain without requiring use of radioactive materials, allowing human volunteers to be studied repeatedly.

Researchers compare ƒMRI, PET, and SPECT scans of depressed patients with those of nondepressed individuals. They also compare scans of individuals before and during specific kinds of brain activity. For instance, which areas of the brain "light up" (i.e., are more active) when individuals with their eyes closed are asked to imagine sad thoughts? Happy thoughts? Do scans reveal consistent abnormalities in brain structure or activity levels in depressed people? Does the image pattern change following successful treatment for depression?

Investigators using various brain imaging techniques have confirmed that frontal lobe abnormalities are implicated in depression, and Ron Duman at Yale, using PET scans, has identified abnormalities in the activity level of the anterior cingulate cortex (fig. 7.1) in depressed patients—another part of the limbic system interconnecting with the frontal lobe.

Post Mortem Studies

Studies on the brains of patients who died from suicide are a major focus of research on depression. The study of post mortem brain tissue is a powerful tool, but the value of the data would be skewed if the brain tissue came from suicide victims who were not depressed at the time of their death. Researchers recognized the weakness in the research model and, in recent years, set up brain banks for research, including the brain collection at Case Western Reserve University, where careful psychiatric scrutiny of suicide victims' records enables researchers to determine which specimens have come from depressed patients and which have come from people whose suicides may have been due to other causes, such as intoxication, terminal illness, personality disorders, or schizophrenia.

Using the Case Western collection, Grazyna Rajkowska at the University of Mississippi Medical Center is comparing the microscopic anatomy of brain tissue in the frontal lobe

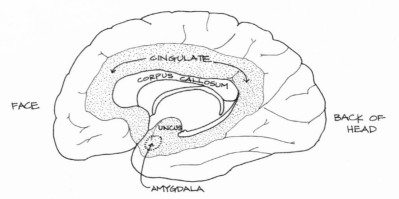

FIG. 7.1. Cingulate cortex of the brain.

of the depressed individuals who died from suicide with similar tissue from the brains of individuals who died from trauma such as motor vehicle accidents or homicides. She has recently documented a decrease in nerve cell size and number in the frontal lobe of the depressed patients, suggesting that the severity of depression may correspond to the areas of the frontal lobe involved from front to back. If the frontal lobes modulate emotional responses as believed, a breakdown in the prefrontal cortex might increase an individual's predisposition to depression.

Many questions are raised by those findings. Is the frontal lobe abnormality developmental or the result of a disease process that causes depression? Are the physical changes in the frontal lobe permanent, or are they reversible with successful treatment of depression? Is the frontal lobe the seat of depression, or does it merely exhibit changes in response to other pathology, perhaps deeper in the brain?

Examination of Living Human Tissue

Researchers continue to examine the relationship of different neurotransmitter levels in the cerebrospinal fluid to the development of depression. One very practical reason for such research is the hope that new and more effective antidepressant medications can be designed. Greg Ordway at the University of Mississippi Medical Center is examining the brains of suicide victims to measure norepinephrine levels and identify changes in structure in the locus coeruleus, a cluster of cells closely associated with norepinephrine production, located in the pons of the brain. Ordway has identified decreased norepinephrine levels and changes in nerve cell size and number in the locus coeruleus of depressed suicide victims. Research has long implicated norepinephrine in the development of depression, but the exact relationship remains obscure and not as straightforward as the close correlation found between the serotonin system and depression.

HPA Axis

The hypothalamic-pituitary-adrenal (HPA) axis has been the subject of intense research in regard to depression. As discussed in chapter 4, corticotropin-releasing factor (CRF) is produced by the hypothalamus and influences the pituitary gland's secretion of corticotropin (ACTH). ACTH, in turn, stimulates the adrenal gland to release cortisol, a steroid that affects many body processes, such as the immune response and glucose metabolism. The HPA axis is activated in response to stress. CRF is increased in the cerebrospinal fluid (CSF) of depressed patients. Initially, it was hoped that measurement of CRF levels in the cerebrospinal fluid might lead to a reliable laboratory test for depression. Recent research, however, has found a great overlap in the levels of CRF in depressed individuals and others, so that CRF levels are not promising as potential laboratory tests for depression.

The HPA axis and CRF, in particular, continue to be active areas for depression research despite the problems with individual variation in the level of CRF in nondepressed people. Researchers have found a decrease in the density of CRF receptors in the frontal cortex of suicide victims, adding further weight to the notion that the frontal lobe is important in the development of depression. It remains unclear as to whether the decrease in the number of CRF receptors in the frontal lobe is cause or effect.

Research currently under way by Garth Bissette at the University of Mississippi Medical Center involves the study of CRF levels in depressed individuals in pre- and posttreatment phases. Previous research by Bissette and colleagues measured CRF levels in depressed patients given electroshock treatment. CRF levels were decreased after electroshock treatment. Bissette's current research follows a similar model using the antidepressant Prozac. Results to date indicate that CRF levels fall after approximately six weeks of treatment. Similar studies (with similar results) that involved use of the antidepressant

Elavil were done by Charles Nemeroff of Emory University
with Dr. Bissette. The studies imply that effective treatment
of depression lowers the level of CRF in the cerebrospinal
fluid. In addition to those who have a purely academic
interest in understanding how the brain works and how
it fails, pharmaceutical companies, eager for the next new
class of antidepressants, are closely watching research on
CRF and hoping that CRF-antagonists may prove to be the
answer.

People have long speculated that exercise may be a good
measure for depression prevention, and recent research (funded
by the National Institute of Mental Health) by Duke University
Medical Center investigators indicates that even sporadic, brief,
vigorous exercise lasting as little as eight minutes may have
significant, although temporary, beneficial effects on depression.
Why is that the case?

Physical exercise is a powerful stimulus to activation of the
HPA axis and is mediated by hypothalamic release of CRF.
As such, it is one of the few noninvasive and effective stimuli
available for use as a provocative test of the HPA axis. At
the present time, the National Institute of Mental Health is
recruiting depressed volunteers for a research project designed
to investigate the HPA axis association between exercise and
mood disorders. The research protocol will study the volunteers'
response to graded exercise levels.

While research has revealed much about the neurochemistry
of depression, we have yet to identify the most basic alteration
in the illness. What makes us think this? The reasoning is that
chemical changes in the body follow quickly after initiation
of antidepressant treatment (medication, light therapy), but
depressive symptoms do not reverse until about six weeks after
treatment is begun. Why the delay in psychological response
after chemical changes occur? Perhaps we are measuring a
secondary change, and we need to look further "upstream" for
the causative factor that alters simultaneously with resolution of
depressive symptoms.

Neurotransmitters, Receptors, and the Synapse

Depression is associated with reductions in brain and spinal fluid neurotransmitter levels, especially serotonin and norepinephrine. Both neurotransmitters are produced in nerve cells and released into the synapse when the nerve cell fires. Afterward, the neurotransmitters are either degraded by enzymes or transported back into the presynaptic neuron (i.e., the nerve cell of origin) and stored in small pools, called vesicles, located within the neuron so that they are available for reuse. The active transport of norepinephrine and serotonin is carried out by specialized cell proteins called transporters. Norepinephrine and serotonin each have different transporter proteins.

Approximately 80 percent of the serotonin released into the synapse is temporarily inactivated by reuptake back into the presynaptic neuron and is available for future release. The reuptake is accomplished by serotonin transporters, proteins that actively transfer serotonin from the synapse across the cell membrane back into the presynaptic neuron and into the neuron's storage vesicles. Research indicates that the brains of depressed humans have markedly decreased numbers of serotonin transporters. Decreased numbers or impaired function of serotonin transporters presumably limits the neuron's ability to recycle serotonin and causes a deficiency of serotonin at its synaptic binding sites, a state which precipitates depressive symptoms.

SSRIs exert their antidepressant effects by blocking the active reuptake of serotonin by its transporters, permitting increased concentrations of the neurotransmitter to activate its synaptic binding sites for an extended period of time. Their action, however, results in less serotonin being returned to the vesicles for later use.

The concentration of serotonin in the synapse is normally regulated by autoreceptors located on the cell membrane of the presynaptic neuron. The autoreceptors signal the nerve cell to produce more serotonin when the neurotransmitter concentration in the synapse is low and to reduce production when the levels are elevated, a process called autoregulation.

Prolonged elevation of serotonin concentration in the synapse appears to cause postsynaptic serotonin receptors to adapt by decreasing their numbers and their sensitivity to serotonin. This process is called down-regulation.

Much current research on depression focuses on the interaction between serotonin and its receptors. Do SSRIs ultimately decrease the amount of serotonin available over time by blocking its reuptake? What effects do medication-induced, prolonged increases in serotonin concentration have on autoregulation of serotonin production and on receptor sensitivity? Are these factors involved in SSRI breakthrough, a recently recognized clinical phenomenon in which depressed patients who initially responded well to SSRIs find themselves again becoming symptomatic while still on their medication?

Laboratory Tests for Depression

Clinicians need a quick, safe, and effective method for diagnosing depression and ruling out other medical illnesses that often simulate depression. Over the years, various laboratory tests for depression have been proposed. Alterations in neurotransmitter levels in the cerebrospinal fluid can be measured, but those laboratory tests are impractical as screening tools in a general population, because a spinal tap is required. A biological marker that can be measured in blood samples would be a more practical test.

One laboratory test, the DST (dexamethasone suppression test), was popular during the 1970s and early 1980s. The DST is based on the observation that the HPA axis is hyperactive in depressed individuals and results in abnormalities in blood levels of serum cortisol which can be measured by a simple blood test. Unfortunately, the DST proved to be less helpful than was initially hoped because the test was not accurate enough, producing falsely negative results in many depressed patients and falsely positive results in some nondepressed individuals.

The search for a blood test for depression continues. One promising avenue is platelet research. Platelets are blood components primarily involved in clotting. Research has shown recently that platelets and neurons have some receptors and proteins that are similar in many respects.

The serotonin transport system in platelets may be abnormal in depression as is the case in brain nerve cells. It is therefore possible that abnormalities of platelet serotonin transporters may serve as an indicator of the same deficiencies in brain nerve cells, potentially allowing for a laboratory test for the diagnosis of depression.

Platelets also have cell membrane receptors for monoamines (such as serotonin and norepinephrine), as do brain nerve cells. Again, investigators are looking at whether abnormalities in brain neuron receptors are mirrored by similar abnormalities in platelet receptors. Angelos Halaris, John Piletz, and their research team at the University of Mississippi Medical Center are on the trail of just such a receptor that can be found on both brain nerve cells and platelets. Although initial results were promising, the investigators must still compare the actions of the receptors from both neurons and platelets and determine whether the receptors mirror one another. If so, their research could also lead to a simple blood test for depression.

Genetic Research

Identifying the genes that play a role in the development of depression is a formidable task, yet that is only the first step in understanding how the genes affect individuals. Genes code for all the proteins that determine physical development (including brain anatomy and function) and behavioral traits. Humans carry an estimated eighty thousand to one hundred thousand genes. A better understanding of the genetics of human development could lead to prevention of gene-based disease.

Abnormal genes associated with depression (primarily of the bipolar type) have been identified in certain families. Researchers in Edinburgh, Scotland, focused their research on a family of more than a hundred individuals, eleven of whom suffered from bipolar disorder. They found strong evidence that the family depression was related to a gene on the short arm of chromosome 4. The same gene was implicated when the study was expanded to include twelve other families. A team at the National Institute of Mental Health (U.S.) looked at 551 genetic markers in affected Amish families, a group popular with geneticists because of their large family size and excellent genealogical records. Their results suggest that three locations—on chromosomes 6, 13, and 15—may carry genes that predispose carriers to depression. Nelson Freimer and colleagues at the University of California at San Francisco examined an isolated population in Costa Rica and found a gene on the long arm of chromosome 18 associated with mood disorder. Other studies implicate genes on chromosome II and the X chromosome. The genetic findings appear to be limited to the families studied and cannot be applied to the general population of depressed individuals. They provide evidence, however, that many different genes can be involved in depression.

If all the genes that cause depression can be identified, clinicians in the future will be better able to counsel couples as to their risk of transmitting to their children a tendency to develop depression.

A new international survey of thirty-eight thousand people from ten countries questions whether genetic hardwiring is the sole determinant of vulnerability to depression. Myrna M. Weismann, a psychologist at Columbia University, and her colleagues found that the rates of major depression in different countries varied by a factor of more than ten. They concluded that cultural differences or risk factors other than genetics may play a significant role in the development of depression. Such research continues to strengthen the position of the fertile ground theory in the development of depression.

Mind-Body Interaction

Suppression of the immune system, as previously noted, has been demonstrated in depressed patients. Depression also negatively affects other body systems.

David Michelson and colleagues at the National Institute of Mental Health demonstrated a loss of hip bone density of such magnitude in women who suffer from major depression as to imply that such women may have as much as a 40 percent higher risk for hip fracture within ten years of onset of the depressive illness.

Dr. Alice Domar of Harvard Medical School has demonstrated the negative effect of depression on another important aspect of women's lives. Her studies show a link between severe depression, stress, and infertility.

Participation in Research

Major depression research centers often rely on human volunteers for critical research. While animal and computerized models serve for the bulk of basic research on the biology of depression, human volunteers are needed to take the research to its ultimate conclusion.

In U.S. and in most international research centers, ethical and scientific guidelines have been developed to protect people who volunteer to participate as subjects in scientific research. All major research centers around the country maintain research committees composed of individuals of varied backgrounds, from researchers to clinicians to ethicists. Not only do the committees review all research proposals for scientific merit and methods, but they also focus carefully on issues of ethics, confidentiality, and safety when human subjects are involved.

Individuals who wish to participate as volunteers in research projects on depression should contact the psychiatry departments in major medical centers and ask for referral to researchers in that field. Major research centers are usually located at university-affiliated medical centers, since academic affiliation is a requirement for funding of research by the National Institute of Mental Health.

Volunteers can also participate in research projects directed by the National Institute of Mental Health. To participate, patients and healthy volunteers must meet certain requirements, which are different for each study.

Patients can request referral to the National Institute of Mental Health by their physicians, who will be asked to supply information on diagnosis and medical history. Physicians can refer a patient to research study at the institute by contacting the patient referral center at the National Institute of Mental Health.

Individuals can also apply directly to the National Institute of Mental Health as patients or as healthy volunteers:

Patient Recruitment and Referral Service, CC.
Quarters 15D-2, 4 West Drive MSC2655
Bethesda, Maryland 20892-2655
Local calls: (301) 496-4891
Out-of-state calls: 1-800-411-1222
Fax: (301) 480-9793
E-mail: prrc@cc.nih.gov

A list of National Institute of Mental Health research projects in need of volunteers and also of referral information is available on the Internet at the following Web site: www.nimh.nih.gov/research/index.htm.

Will depression one day go the way of smallpox? Our hope lies in the efforts of dedicated scientists and a citizenry willing to fund basic research and science education.

Appendix A: Sources of Additional Information

This appendix contains a list of organizations, mailing addresses, Web sites, and recommended readings providing additional information and support for depressives and those who care about them.

Organizations

The National Alliance for the Mentally Ill (NAMI)
200 North Glebe Road, Suite 1015
Arlington, VA 22203-3754
www.nami.org

A nationwide self-help, support, and advocacy organization with state and local affiliates that provides the public with information on mental illness, including discussions of types of mental illness, advances in treatment, legal perspectives, and government actions.

NAMI Helpline
1-800-950-NAMI

A toll-free information and referral service, manned by volunteers, which provides emotional support, referrals to local organizations, and treatment information.

Bipolar Network News
Published by the Stanley Foundation Bipolar Network (a joint project of NAMI and NIMH).
To subscribe, call 1-800-518-7326 or write to:

Bipolar Network News
c/o Stanley Foundation
5430 Grosvenor Lane, Suite #200
Bethesda, MD 20814
Fax: 301-571-0768
E-mail: stanley@sparky.nimh.nih.gov
    A free publication for people who suffer from bipolar disorder or have family members with the illness.

American Association of Retired Persons (AARP)
Widowed Persons Service
601 E Street, N.W.
Washington, DC 20049
202-434-2260
    A component of the well-known parent organization that focuses on psychosocial needs of widowed people, including those with depression.

National Depressive and Manic-Depressive Association
    (NDMDA)
730 N. Franklin
Suite 501
Chicago, IL 60610
1-800-826-3632
www.ndmda.org/index.html
    An association that provides information on depressive illnesses to the public.

National Mental Health Association (NMHA)
1021 Prince Street
Alexandria, VA 22314-2971
1-800-433-5959
1-800-969-NMHA
www.nmha.org
    An organization of community mental health centers that provides information on mental health issues to the public.

DEPRESSION Awareness, Recognition, and Treatment
(D/ART) Program
National Institute of Mental Health
5600 Fishers Lane
Room 15C-05
Rockville, MD 20857
1-800-421-4211
One of the NIMH programs dedicated to advancing the
understanding and treatment of depression.

Survivors of Suicide (SOS)
A self-help support group with local chapters designed to
help adult family members and friends who have lost a loved
one to suicide. Phone numbers can be found in local phone
directories.

The Campaign on Clinical Depression
1-800-228-1114
A program of the National Mental Health Association.

National Depression Screening Project
1-800-573-4433
Call to locate a free confidential screening site near you.

Society for Light Treatment and Biological Rhythms
10200 W. 44 Ave.
Wheat Ridge, CO 80033-2840
303-424-3697
A group that helped establish the guidelines and standards
for light therapy in SAD.

Other Web Sites Providing Information on Depression

American Medical Association
www.ama-assn.org/consumer/specond.htm

American Psychiatric Association
www.psych.org

American Psychological Association
www.apa.org

Depression.com
www.depression.com

Doctor's Guide to Depression Information and Resources
www.pslgroup.com/DEPRESSION.HTM

Internet Mental Health
www.mentalhealth.com

Mediconsult.com
www.mediconsult.com/depression

Mental Health InfoSource
www.mhsource.com

Mental Health Net
www.cmhc.com

National Association for Research on Schizophrenia and
Depression
www.mhsource.com/disorders/depress.html

National Institute of Mental Health (NIMH)
www.nimh.nih.gov

Society for Light Treatment and Biological Rhythms
www.websciences.org/sltbr

Recommended Reading

Beck, Aaron T. *Cognitive Therapy and the Emotional Disorders.*
New York: Meridian, 1979.
    An early and very readable book about cognitive approaches
to dealing with emotional disorders.

Beck, Judith S. *Cognitive Therapy: Basics and Beyond.* New York:
The Guilford Press, 1995.
    A very good book describing basic concepts of cognitive
therapy.

Brando, Marlon, with Robert Lindsay. *Brando: Songs My Mother
Taught Me.* New York: Random House, 1994.
    An autobiographical account of actor Marlon Brando's
struggle with emotions, including depression and rage.

Burns, D. *Feeling Good: The New Mood Therapy.* New York:
Signet, 1980.
    A self-help guide for treating depression through the
use of cognitive therapy; includes charts and homework
assignments and gives indicators for need of professional
treatment.

Copeland, Mary Ellen. *The Depression Workbook: A Guide for
Living with Depression and Manic Depression.* Oakland, CA:
New Harbinger Publications, 1992.
    A book based on cognitive behavior treatment methods for
depression.

Cronkite, Kathy. *On the Edge of Darkness: Conversations about
Conquering Depression.* New York: Doubleday, 1994.
    An account by newsman Walter Cronkite's daughter,
featuring a variety of personal stories by her and by celebrities
about their experiences with depression.

Duke, Patty (Anna Pearce), with Kenneth Duran. *Call Me Anna: The Autobiography of Patty Duke*. New York: Bantam Books, 1987.

The autobiography of Patty Duke, who suffered from manic-depression.

Duke, Patty (Anna Pearce), and Gloria Hochman. *A Brilliant Madness: Living with Manic Depressive Illness*. New York: Bantam Books, 1992.

An autobiographical account of actress Patty Duke's struggle with manic-depression, with alternate chapters written by Gloria Hochman describing the clinical features of the illness.

Fieve, Ronald R. *Moodswing*. New York: Bantam Books, 1989.

A good discussion of bipolar disorder and its treatment.

———. *Prozac: Questions and Answers for Patients, Family and Physicians*. New York: Avon, 1996.

A discussion of depression and the medications used to treat the illness.

Gabbard, Glen O. *Psychodynamic Psychiatry in Clinical Practice*. Washington, DC: American Psychiatric Press, Inc., 1994.

A detailed discussion of the principles of psychodynamic psychotherapy.

Gurman, Alan S., and Stanley B. Messer. *Essential Psychotherapies*. New York: The Guilford Press, 1995.

A good review, comparing and contrasting major forms of psychotherapy.

Hartley, Mariette. *Breaking the Silence*. New York: Putnam, 1990.

An autobiographical account of actress Mariette Hartley's efforts to deal with the suicide of her father and of her advocacy work in preventing suicide.

Jamison, Kay Redfield. *Touched with Fire*. New York: Free Press Paperbacks, 1993.
   A discussion of bipolar illness and the artistic temperament.

―――. *An Unquiet Mind: A Memoir of Moods and Madness*. New York: Vintage Books, 1996.
   An autobiographical account of a clinician's descent into and recovery from bipolar illness.

Morrison, J. M. *Your Brother's Keeper*. Chicago: Nelson-Hall Publications, 1981.
   Practical advice for families regarding the treatment of mood disorders.

Papolos, Demitri F., M.D., and Janice Papolos. *Overcoming Depression*. New York: Harper Collins, 1992.
   A compendium of current knowledge about the causes and treatments of mood disorders, including summaries of the latest research.

Styron, William. *Darkness Visible: A Memoir of Madness*. New York: Vintage Books, 1992.
   A description of the novelist's own experience with depression and recovery.

Thompson, Tracy. *Beast (The): A Reckoning with Depression*. New York: Putnam and Sons, 1995.
   An autobiographical account of reporter Tracy Thompson's battles with depression.

Wurtzel, Elizabeth. *Prozac Nation: Young and Depressed in America*. New York: Houghton Mifflin Company, 1994.
   A very readable book about the author's battle with depression.

Appendix B: Medications

Antidepressants

These medications are used primarily in the treatment of depression, although they can also be prescribed for other disorders, such as chronic pain, panic disorder, and attention deficit disorder.

Monoamine Oxidase Inhibitors

The first widely used class of antidepressants, these medications are effective, but can cause life-threatening hypertensive crises if combined with certain other medications (prescription and over-the-counter) or with certain foods that contain tyramine. While these medications are still in use, they are no longer the first line of treatment and are not commonly prescribed.

Generic Name	*Brand Name*
tranylcypromine	Parnate
phenelzine	Nardil
isocarboxazid	Marplan

Tricyclics

The most widely used class of antidepressants in the United States from the 1950s until the late 1980s, these medications are effective but produce many side effects, including dry mouth, constipation, increased appetite and weight gain, blurred vision, sedation, abnormalities of heart rhythm, confusion, and drops in blood pressure when a patient stands. They are often lethal in overdose.

Generic Name	*Brand Name*
amitriptyline	Elavil
	Endep
imipramine	Tofranil
doxepin	Sinequan
	Adapin
protriptyline	Vivactil
desipramine	Norpramin
	Pertofrane
nortriptyline	Pamelor
	Aventyl
trimipramine	Surmontil
clomipramine	Anafranil

Miscellaneous

Not chemically related to one another, these medications are effective antidepressants but have unique side effects that limit their use.

Generic Name	*Brand Name*
amoxapine	Asendin
maprotyline	Ludiomil
trazodone	Desyrel
buproprion	Wellbutrin

Selective Serotonin Reuptake Inhibitors (SSRIs)

Currently the most widely used class of antidepressants, these medications are effective and have relatively few side effects, including headache, indigestion, diarrhea, initial weight loss followed by weight gain later in therapy, agitation, insomnia, and decreased sexual drive and performance. To date, these medications have been relatively safe in overdose.

Generic Name	*Brand Name*
fluoxetine	Prozac
sertraline	Zoloft

paroxetine	Paxil
fluvoxamine	Luvox
citalopram	Celexa

Recent Additions

Sharing some characteristics with SSRIs, these antidepressants differ from each other in chemical structure, mechanisms of action, and side effect profiles.

Generic Name	*Brand Name*
nefazodone	Serzone
venlafaxine	Effexor
mirtazapine	Remeron

Stimulants

Prescribed primarily for the treatment of narcolepsy (a sleep disorder) and attention deficit disorder, these medications may be effective as supplemental treatments for treatment-resistant depression.

Generic Name	*Brand Name*
dextroamphetamine	Dexedrine
methylphenidate	Ritalin
pemoline	Cylert
amphetamine combination	Adderall

Mood Stabilizers

These medications, many of which are anticonvulsants (antiseizure medicines), are effective in the treatment of some patients with mood swing disorders. The newest of these (the three listed last) are now prescribed in treatment-resistant mood swing disorders when other mood stabilizers are ineffective.

Generic Name	*Brand Name*
lithium carbonate	Eskalith
	Lithobid
carbamazepine	Tegretol
valproic acid	Depakote
gabapentin	Neurontin
lamotrogine	Lamictal
topiramate	Topamax

Glossary

Acetylcholine (Ach) A neurotransmitter active in both the peripheral and the central nervous system.

Adrenal glands A pair of small glands that sit atop the kidneys and produce several hormones, including those produced in response to stressful conditions.

Amygdala A cluster of specialized nerve cells lying deep in each hemisphere of the brain that constitutes an evolutionarily primitive nerve center and plays an important role in emotions.

Antidepressants A group of medications of differing chemical properties that are used primarily to elevate mood toward normal in the treatment of depressive illness.

Asphyxiation Usually refers to death from inability to breathe ("smothering").

Assortive mating The tendency for males and females of similar traits and tendencies to pair (and produce offspring).

Atypical bipolar disorder A mood swing disorder with both abnormal mood elevations and abnormal mood depressions occurring in a pattern other than that classically described for bipolar disorder.

Aversive techniques Methods utilizing administration of a painful, noxious, or otherwise unwelcome stimulus as a way to induce the subject to change behavior.

Bereavement Commonly used to refer to the loss of a loved one through death.

Bipolar disorder A mood swing disorder characterized by episodes of both mania and depression, classically with intervening periods of normal mood.

Brain stem The portion of the central nervous stem that connects the spinal cord with the brain and contains many nerve centers (nuclei) regulating primitive brain functions, such as arousal.

Cardioversion A medical procedure utilizing application of brief electrical discharges to the chest wall in order to reset the pacing mechanism of the heart from a potentially lethal rhythm to a normal rhythm.

Cerebrospinal fluid (CSF) The body fluid that bathes and protects the central nervous system (the brain and spinal cord) and serves as a transport medium carrying gases (such as oxygen and carbon dioxide), nutrients, antibodies, and medications to cells of the central nervous system and removing waste materials from the central nervous system.

Cerebellum A large, oval part of the brain that lies in the skull behind the brain stem and midbrain and beneath the back portions of the cerebrum; coordinates muscle tone, posture, and eye and hand movements on the basis of sensory information received from other parts of the brain and the body; may also have coordinating effects involving more subtle cognitive functions of the brain.

Cerebrum The major portion of the brain, composed of two halves (joined by the corpus callosum), each with four lobes; forms the largest part of the central nervous system in humans; contains the centers for control of speech, motor activity, sensory reception, emotion, and various cognitive functions, such as calculation, memory, planning, and judgment.

Circadian Cyclical variations of approximately twenty-four hours in biochemical and physiological functions and levels of activity.

Cognition A relatively high level of information processing by the brain, including memory, calculation, perceiving, and "thinking" processes.

Cognitive Referring to cognition.

Compulsion A repetitive, irrational, and often trivial motor act or ritual that an individual feels compelled to perform despite wishing not to do so.

Compulsive Describing an individual who is prone to compulsions or a behavior that is performed because of an internal urge despite the individual's wish not to do so.

Computerized tomography (CT) A method of body scanning that yields images of anatomy rather than activity level, often used to detect abnormalities of structure within the brain.

Connective tissue Body tissue that binds together and is the ground substance of the various parts and organs of the body.

Corpus callosum A broad white-matter tract deep within the brain that connects the two cerebral hemispheres together and allows transfer of information between the two.

Cortex, cerebral The outer layer of the brain; usually refers specifically to the outer layer of the cerebrum.

Cortisol A hormone produced by the adrenal cortex that affects the metabolism of glucose, protein, and fats and is often increased in response to stress.

Cortisone A natural hormone that is converted in the body to cortisol; used as an anti-inflammatory and immunosuppressant agent and for adrenal hormone replacement therapy.

Delusion A false belief that is firmly maintained despite evidence to the contrary and is not shared by the culture.

Dementia A cognitive disorder with defects in memory, judgment, orientation, emotional reactivity, concentration, and ability to initiate and maintain organized behavior; usually chronic, but some forms may be reversible.

Demyelination Destruction, removal, or loss of the protective myelin (lipid-rich) sheath that surrounds a nerve or nerves.

Deoxyribonucleic acid (DNA) The chemical that makes up the primary genetic material of all cellular organisms and certain viruses, located in the nucleus of the cell as the double-helix of chromosomes on which are contained the genes that code for the development of the organism and its physiological activities.

Depression A clinical syndrome with lowering of mood, loss of pleasure capacity, changes in sleep, appetite, and sexual interest, decreased activity level, and reversible changes in cognitive function including problems with memory and concentration; in severe cases, may be associated with loss of contact with reality as evidenced by delusions and hallucinations.

Detoxification The process of withdrawal from addicting substances, usually under medical supervision; known colloquially as "detox."

Diabetes mellitus A metabolic disorder of glucose metabolism caused by a disturbance in the normal insulin mechanism that can lead to serious illness, coma, and death.

Dopamine A neurotransmitter in the central nervous system and an intermediate product in the synthesis of norepinephrine.

Double depression A term used to describe the simultaneous presence of two distinct depressive syndromes in the same individual; usually referring to an episode of severe clinical depression overlying a chronic, milder depressive disorder.

Down syndrome An inherited syndrome of mental retardation associated with distinctive physical alterations caused by an abnormality in the pairing of chromosome 21.

Dysthymia A mild-to-moderate depressive state, usually chronic in nature but not severe enough to be a major depression.

Dysthymic disorder The term used by the *Diagnostic and Statistical Manual* (*DSM-IV*), produced by the American Psychiatric Association, to describe a mild-to-moderate depressive disorder (dysthymia) persisting more days than not for at least two years.

Ego A term used by Freud (and in psychoanalytically oriented psychology) to describe one of the three divisions of the personality dominated by the reality principle; the division that mediates between the needs and desires of the individual and the realities of the individual's environment (the other two divisions being the id and the superego).

Ego ideal That part of the ego that develops parental images, or role models.

Electrocardiogram (EKG or **ECG)** A medical procedure by which the electrical discharges associated with heart beating are measured via electrodes placed on the chest wall and graphically displayed; often used to detect heart pacing abnormalities and abnormalities of electrical conduction in the nerve fibers of the heart and the heart muscle, such as those caused by compromised blood flow from coronary artery disease or from myocardial infarction (heart attack).

Electroconvulsive therapy (ECT) A medical procedure utilizing application of brief electrical discharges under controlled conditions via an electrode or a pair of electrodes placed on the front portion of the head in order to induce a seizure, thereby alleviating the symptoms of certain specific psychiatric disorders, in particular, severe depression; also known as electroshock therapy (EST).

Electroencephalography (EEG) A medical procedure by which the electrical discharges associated with brain activity are measured via electrodes placed on the scalp and graphically represented; often used to detect seizure activity or to determine brain death.

Emote To exhibit emotion.

Empathy The ability to comprehend another person's emotions in response to his or her reality.

Endocrine glands Glands in the human body that secrete hormones affecting the function of other parts of the body.

Endorphin Any of three neuropeptides that are amino acid residues of ß-lipotropin (ß=beta) and that bind to opiate receptors in various areas of the brain to produce a potent analgesic effect.

Enkephalin Either of two pentapeptides that are found in the brain, spinal cord, and gastrointestinal tract and that have potent opiate-like effects and serve as neurotransmitters in the central nervous system.

Enzyme A protein that serves as a catalyst to induce chemical reactions in other substances without itself being altered or destroyed by the process.

Epidemiology The study of the relationships of various factors determining the frequency and distribution of diseases in the human population.

Estrogen A sex hormone produced in females.

Euphoria A mood state of extreme elation; when sustained, often associated with bipolar disorder or with substance abuse.

Executive functions The higher functions of the cognitive process, such as those involving initiation, planning, and maintenance of activities and appropriateness of behavior; the center for executive cognitive functions is located in the frontal lobes.

Familial The tendency for a trait to appear in multiple biologically related family members; such a trait is said to "run in the family."

Frontal lobe One of the four lobes of each cerebral hemisphere—the front portion, containing nerve centers that are involved in executive cognitive functions including abstract thinking, memory, mood, voluntary control of skeletal muscles, and speech.

GABA γ-aminobutyric acid (γ=gamma); a neurotransmitter.

Gray matter The cerebral cortex.

Hallucination A false perception caused by abnormal brain function such as that found in psychotic disorders or caused by substance abuse; may be visual, auditory, olfactory (smell), gustatory (taste), somatic (internal), or tactile (touch).

Huntington's chorea A hereditary, degenerative central nervous system disorder causing progressive deterioration in cognitive and motor function, resulting in dementia, severe movement disorders, and eventually death.

Hypersomnia Excessive drowsiness or sleep.

Hyperthyroidism Overactivity of the thyroid gland resulting in excessive production of thyroid hormone, usually causing abnormal functioning of other body organs, including the brain.

Hypomania A mild form of mania.

Hypothalamus A structure deep within the brain that is composed of multiple nerve centers coordinating and transmitting information to and from other parts of the brain; operates in many "feedback loops" to regulate brain activity and the production of body hormones, including feedback mechanisms involving the pituitary gland, the thyroid gland, the adrenal glands, and the gonads (sex glands).

Hypothyroidism Underactivity of the thyroid gland resulting in low production of thyroid hormone, usually causing abnormal functioning of other body organs, including the brain.

Id A term used by Freud (and in psychoanalytically oriented psychology) to describe the one of the three divisions of the personality that is completely unconscious (i.e., the individual is unaware of its existence) and primitive; comprises the needs, desires, and drives of the individual (the other two divisions being the ego and the superego).

Insight Self-understanding; knowledge of the objective reality of a situation; used in psychiatry to describe the patient's knowledge that the symptoms of his or her illness are abnormal.

Insomnia Inability to sleep.

Interpersonal Referring to interaction between two or more individuals; in psychiatric literature, often refers to a specialized form of psychotherapy that involves dealing with role disputes, role changes, grief, and other relationship problems.

Introspection The process of analyzing one's own beliefs, emotions, and motivations.

Introversion Preoccupation with oneself; also used to describe a tendency to be shy or bashful.

Involutional melancholia A term once used to describe a severe depression first occurring in midlife.

Libido A term used by Freud (and in psychoanalytically oriented psychology) to describe the energy of the sexual drive.

Light therapy A treatment for seasonal affective disorder (SAD) utilizing exposure of affected individuals to light; also known as phototherapy.

Limbic system An interrelated circuit of deep brain structures involved in emotion, behavior, autonomic functions, and olfaction.

ß-Lipotropin (ß=beta) A polypeptide synthesized by the anterior portion of the pituitary gland which promotes fat mobilization and skin darkening; a precursor of endorphins.

Magnetic resonance imaging (MRI) A method of body imaging or scanning, often used to detect abnormalities of structure within the brain.

Mania Sustained, abnormal elevation of mood found in bipolar disorder and often associated with poor insight, paranoia, grandiosity, hyperactivity, insomnia, poor judgment, and sometimes hallucinations.

Manic-depressive illness The term formerly used to denote the mood swing disorder now called bipolar disorder.

Medulla The pyramid-shaped portion of the brain lying between and connecting the nerve tracts of the spinal cord and the pons; part of the brain stem.

Melancholia An older term used to describe the illness now called depression.

Melatonin A neurotransmitter produced by the pineal gland, synthesized from serotonin, and involved with regulation of biological rhythms, such as sleep, mood, puberty, and ovarian cycles.

Menopause The cessation of menses; the phase of life when females go through a transition from the early adult period of reproductive capacity to the late adult state of infertility, involving gradual and sporadic decreases in female hormones that produce both transient and permanent body symptoms, often including cessation of menses, changes in bone density, and mood changes.

Metabolism The biophysiological processes by which living cells and tissues undergo the continuous chemical changes necessary for life and reproduction.

Metastatic Referring to spread of a malignancy (cancer) from its initial or primary location to other areas of the body.

Midbrain The portion of the brain lying between the pons and the cerebral hemispheres; plays a role in control of eye movements, in motor control of skeletal muscles, and in relay of auditory and visual systems.

Monoamine oxidase An enzyme located in the central nervous system as well as in other parts of the body that degrades monoamines (such as serotonin and norepinephrine).

Monoamine oxidase inhibitor (MAOI) A medication that blocks the action of the enzyme monoamine oxidase; often used to treat depression.

Mood swing disorder Commonly used synonymously with the term "bipolar disorder."

Musculoskeletal Referring to the system of muscles and skeleton.

Mutation An unpredictable change in a gene or group of genes that may affect the development of an organism and produce alterations in the trait(s) of a living organism; many mutations are lethal.

Narcolepsy A sleep disorder that results in recurrent, uncontrollable, brief episodes of sleep during the day.

Neurological Referring to functions of both the central and peripheral nervous systems.

Neurohormonal Hormones produced by structures of the brain, such as the pituitary gland and the pineal gland.

Neurotransmitter Chemicals that function in the nervous system as part of the process that transmits information from one neuron to the next.

Nihilism The delusion of nonexistence; it may refer only to parts of the world, to the self, or to everything.

Norepinephrine A monoamine that serves as a neurotransmitter in the central nervous system.

Obsession A persistent, unwelcome emotion, idea, or impulse that repetitively and insistently forces itself into one's consciousness and that cannot be eliminated by reasoning.

Obsessive-compulsive disorder A psychiatric disorder manifested by the presence of obsessions and compulsions.

Occipital lobe One of the four lobes of each cerebral hemisphere—the back portion, containing nerve centers that are involved in visual function.

Optic nerve The collection of nerve fibers that transfers visual information from the retina of the eye to the "visual" cortex of the occipital lobe of the brain.

Orbital area The portion of the frontal lobe located behind the "orbits" of the eyes.

Osteoporosis A disorder of calcium loss from the bones resulting in decreased strength of the bones.

Paleobrain The portion of the brain that houses nerve centers involved in the primitive, basic life functions regulated by the brain; does not include the cerebral cortex.

Pancreas The organ of the body that produces insulin and digestive enzymes.

Paranoia A delusion (persistent, pervasive false belief) that other individuals or forces are purposefully working to cause harm.

Paranoid Refers to a delusional idea or to a person who harbors a delusion of paranoia.

Parietal lobe One of the four lobes of each cerebral hemisphere— the top midportion, between the frontal lobe and the occipital lobe, containing nerve centers that are involved in a number of complex cognitive activities, including sensory functions (sensations of touch, heat, position), the ability to recognize people and objects, and the ability to recognize and use patterns of language and numbers.

Phototherapy A treatment for seasonal affective disorder (SAD) utilizing exposure of affected individuals to light; also known as light therapy.

Physiology The basic chemical processes of life and reproduction; the science that deals with the chemical and biological functions of the living organism and its parts.

Pituitary gland A gland located on the underside of the brain that produces neurohormones that assist in the regulation of hormone production by other glands of the body, including the thyroid gland, the adrenal gland, and the gonads (sex glands).

Polysomnography A test used to monitor brain, respiratory, and skeletal muscle activity during sleep.

Pons The portion of the brain located between the medulla and the midbrain and in front of the cerebellum; contains nerve centers involved with regulation of basic life functions, including blood pressure and breathing, as well as with the relay of information from the cerebral hemispheres to the cerebellum.

Positron emission tomography (PET) A method of body scanning using mildly radioactive compounds to yield images of activity level rather than precise anatomy; often used to detect abnormalities of function of the structures within the brain.

Postmenopausal The phase of life in a woman following menopause.

Postpartum The period of time (days to a few weeks) following childbirth.

Prefrontal The front portion of the frontal lobe of the brain.

Prepubertal The phase of life (childhood) before the onset of reproductive fertility (puberty) in adolescence.

Progesterone A female sex hormone.

Pseudodementia A syndrome of decreased cognitive function (such as memory, concentration, ability to process information rapidly and accurately) in which the symptoms of cognitive degeneration are typical of dementia but are instead caused by severe depression and resolve with successful treatment of the depression.

Psychodynamic Related to the science of how mental forces interact to adapt to life.

Psychosis A state of severe brain malfunction associated with delusions and hallucinations; found in severe forms of psychiatric disorders, such as schizophrenia, bipolar disorder, dementia, and acute substance abuse.

Psychotherapy Treatment of psychiatric disorders through verbal communication.

Puberty The phase of life, usually in adolescence, when reproductive fertility and physical changes consistent with maleness and femaleness begin.

Quadraplegia Paralysis of all four extremities.

Rapid cycling A frequency of bipolar mood swings of at least four per year.

Rapid eye movement (REM) stage of sleep One of five stages of sleep based on level of brain activity as reflected by EEG patterns and motor function of the body; the stage of sleep in which the eyes move rapidly beneath closed lids but the body does not move; the stage of dreaming.

Receptors A protein component on the surface of nerve cells that binds with a specific neurotransmitter to induce a response within the nerve cell.

Reinforcement Reward for a behavior that tends to increase the chances of the behavior continuing or occurring again.

Remission A medical term for disappearance of symptoms of illness.

Replication The process by which organisms reproduce, usually referring to the asexual reproduction of bacteria and viruses.

Retina The interior lining of the eye; contains the receptors for light and images that transmit the information to the optic nerve.

Ribonucleic acid (RNA) Genetic material found in the cells of living organisms and certain viruses; serves as a template on which the cell builds its master genes, deoxyribonucleic acid (DNA).

Schizophrenia A psychiatric disorder of psychotic, disorganized processing of thoughts and emotions which results in illogical thinking and speech, mood changes, development of delusions, and hallucinations (predominantly auditory, but can also include visual, tactile, and somatic).

Seasonal affective disorder (SAD) A mood disorder with mood swings occurring predictably at certain seasons of the year, usually fall to winter and/or spring.

Seropositive Refers to a positive result from a blood test for one of various medical disorders, including, for example, syphilis, acquired immune deficiency syndrome, and hepatitis.

Serotonin A monoamine that serves as a neurotransmitter in the central nervous system.

Shock treatment A common term for the medical procedure electoshock (or electroconvulsive) treatment.

Single photon emission computed tomography (SPECT) A method of body scanning in which mildly radioactive compounds yield images of activity level rather than precise anatomy; often used to detect abnormalities of function of the structures within the brain.

SSRI Selective serotonin reuptake inhibitor; a class of antidepressant medication.

Stereotypy A repeated movement that does not appear to be goal-directed and is more complex than the simple movement of a muscular tic.

Steroids A class of hormones (including cortisone) that can be synthetically produced; used to treat a variety of medical disorders, including inflammatory conditions such as arthritis.

Substance P An II-amino acid peptide present in nerve cells scattered throughout the body; increases the contraction of gastrointestinal smooth muscle, causes dilatation of blood vessels, serves as a sensory neurotransmitter especially for pain, and may be a factor in depression.

Superego A term used by Freud (and in psychoanalytically oriented psychology) to describe one of the three divisions of the personality; it is mainly unconscious and comprises the conscience (the other two divisions being the ego and the id).

Synapse (synaptic cleft) The area between the end of one nerve cell and the beginning of another, at which point impulses are transmitted from one cell to the next; neurotransmitters are extruded from a cell and diffuse into the space, binding with the receptor sites and inducing a response in the receiving cell.

Temporal lobe One of the four lobes of each cerebral hemisphere—the lateral or side portion, containing nerve centers that are involved in mood, memory, speech, hearing, smelling, vision, and learning.

Therapeutic Producing healing effects.

Thyroid gland A gland located in the neck in front of the trachea (windpipe) and producing a hormone that regulates the activity of other body functions, including functions of the brain.

Transcranial magnetic stimulation (TMS) An experimental procedure used to identify functions of specific parts of the brain; involves exposure of different areas of the brain to magnetic fields generated by a magnet held to portions of the scalp and causing changes in the magnetic fields of the underlying areas of the brain, stimulating increased activity in those areas.

Tricyclic A class of antidepressant medications.

Ultradian Pertaining to a biological rhythm with a period of fewer than twenty-four hours; more recently used to refer to ultrarapid cycling of mood that can occur within less than a day and is associated with a severe form of bipolar disorder.

Ultraviolet light Slow light wave forms outside the visual range of humans.

Unconscious drives A term used by Freud (and in psychoanalytically oriented psychology) to refer to desires and needs that are outside the individual's awareness but which motivate his or her behavior.

White matter The inner portion of the cerebrum beneath the cortex, or gray matter.

Index